Biblical Demonology
Their Origins and Unwilling Role in Sanctification
By Anthony Uyl MTS

Devoted Publishing
Ingersoll, Ontario. Canada 2022

Biblical Demonology: Their Origins and Unwilling Role in Sanctification

By Anthony Uyl MTS

Cover and Paper Background designs done by Zsuzsa Fige and are the property of 2165467 Ontario Inc.

ISBN: 978-1-77356-434-0

The text of Biblical Demonology: Their Origins and Unwilling Role in Sanctification is all protected under Copyright ©2022 Devoted Publishing. The covers, background, layout and Devoted Publishing logo are Copyright ©2022 Devoted Publishing. This edition is published by Devoted Publishing a division of 2165467 Ontario Inc.

Scripture quotations are from the ESV® Bible (The Holy Bible, English Standard Version®), copyright © 2001 by Crossway, a publishing ministry of Good News Publishers. Used by permission. All rights reserved. The ESV text may not be quoted in any publication made available to the public by a Creative Commons license. The ESV may not be translated into any other language.

All other direct quotations fall under "Fair Use" guidelines as defined on the publishers' website. The use of these quotations does not automatically allow a reader to quote the material directly from this book as "Fair Use." Since there are no "Fair Use" regulations in Canada, any use of original material within this publication does not fall under "Fair Use." Unless written permission is given for any quoted original material, all use of this material to be reproduced, stored in a retrieval system, or transmitted in any form by any means, electronic, mechanical, photocopying, recording or otherwise is forbidden. All rights reserved.

Contact Us Online:
Email: office@devotedpub.com
Facebook: @devotedpublishing
Authors' Twitter: @AnthonyUyl
For more information on Biblical Demonology and issues with the occult in modern evangelicalism, check out the authors' Substack Blog Reformed Demonology: reformeddemonology.substack.com

Table of Contents

Forward...	v
Prologue...	vii
Chapter I – Introduction..	1
Chapter II - Origins of the Demonic..................................	5
Chapter III - The Testing of Job (Job 1-2:10, Job 42)................	19
Chapter IV - Peter, and the Apostles, being "sifted like wheat"..... (Luke 22:31-38)	27
Excursus...	31
Chapter V - God Allows a Spirit to Test to Condemn (1 Kings..... 22:13-28)	33
Chapter VI - God Forbids that Satan Accuse the High Priest........ (Zechariah 3)	37
Chapter VII - The Testing of the Church in History..................	41
Chapter VIII – Conclusion...	45
Epilogue...	xi
Appendix - "I rebuke you Satan in Jesus' name!" ... wait ... is..... this biblical?	xiii
Bibliography..	xix
Recommended Books...	xxiv

Forward

Over the history of the church there has been an overemphasis on the demonic at various times and among various groups. In our day it has been present not only in charismatic and Pentecostal churches but also in some non charismatic contexts. Whenever there is an emphasis on the demonic the focus of the church is less on Christ and more on demons. This is a great concern and should trouble any follower of Christ. It should also be a concern for evangelicals who hold to the authority of the Bible because there is almost nothing prescribed in scripture instructing us in dealing with the demonic. Yes, Jesus and the apostles did cast out demons, but only out of possessed non-believers, and never out of New Covenant believers. In the New Covenant believers are told to resist the devil and put on the armour of God, not to fight him with words or to cast out demons who are oppressing believers. I am not saying that believers are not at times oppressed with temptations. The devil and his demons are concerned with making believers stumble in sin and forsake Christ. If this is the case, the church should not be concerned with delivering the believer from the supposed demon of pride, lust, greed, depression, etc. If a person is suffering from one of these sins, they need to go to their pastor who can provide biblical counselling.

My concern is that in our postmodern, experiential culture, this focus on the demonic is actually meeting some psychological need of its practitioners and patients, and borders on spiritualism which we are commanded to flee from.

For these reasons I appreciate Anthony Uyl's book, Biblical Demonology: Their Origins and Unwilling Role in Sanctification. Uyl looks at several important passages in the Old and New Testaments where we see the testing of God's people by demons. He uses the examples of Job, the lying spirit in the prophet Micaiah to Ahab, the vision of the high priest in Zechariah, as well as a brief survey of Church history. He shows that our sovereign God uses the demons for his purposes and, in particular, for the purpose of the sanctification of his people. God's desire is for our sanctification which means mortifying the flesh and putting on Christ. This is what the devil hates and seeks to destroy in the believer. Instead of focusing our attention on the invisible spirit world, we should be focussing on Christ through His word and Spirit. I wonder if this focus on demons is actually Satan's strategy to get our focus away from Christ and instead on ourselves. I think it could very well be.

I highly recommend that you read Anthony Uyl's book and from it see that our God is sovereign over all things including the demonic world, and uses it for our sake, even our sanctification, and His glory. Soli Deo Gloria.

- Dr. Barry Howson

Prologue

People will often ask me what got me into studying biblical demonology. I always kind of smirk because I know for certain the answer is not one they are either going to like or believe.

I will not bore you with the details, however, every Christian demonologist has a starting point, and it is not always a good one. What shows a test of how Godly of a person they are is whether they focus all attention on the demonic or take the time to realize how God really is and the gift of grace through Christ that God has given us. When Christian demonologists become too focused on the affairs of darkness, it can have detrimental effects to that poor students' emotional and spiritual life. While I am not going to say that this is a field everyone should delve into, those that are interested in these studies, need to find people to be accountable to. Not family or close friends, I am talking elders and senior leaders of a local biblical and gospel preaching church.

This book originally was submitted as a Seminary research paper that I had to write to graduate with my Masters. There is some writing in this version that was not in the original. I wanted to include the added material, but my project advisor was very adamant that the paper was to be no more than fifty pages. By the end of writing and editing, if I had hit my enter key one more time, I would have been on page fifty-one.

While many are looking at disgust at this type of study, what is happening in many churches around the world shows the need for someone that is specializing in this area. The Reformed/Calvinist side of the theological persuasions are surprisingly lacking in any theological study when it comes to demonology. The attitudes for this are many and will not be summarized here. What has ended up happening is a number of "spiritual warfare" and "deliverance" ministries from the extreme charismatic side of the church are writing material that is quite honestly, far from a proper biblical exegesis. Some of these books have stated things that are plainly against the testimony of the Bible about faith, salvation, even the power of Christ to free someone from demonic oppression.

In reading some of these books for various studies, what I have seen is the ritualization of "deliverance" sessions where other Christians doing specific things that are in no way ever spoken of biblically, or even suggested as liturgical for everyday practice, that are required for the "deliverance" to happen. All of this has happened, I believe, because people have relied too much on the existential to define their biblical truth rather than acting on presuppositions that the Bible is true simply because it is the word of God. Additional spiritual things that we discover through our existential moments should not in any way be ever read into the biblical testimony. Yet, many of these extreme charismatics that are writing these spiritual warfare books are doing just that. Experience overrides the Bible.

I started trying to deal with a lot of emotional problems I suffered from, just from the fact that it was a part of my biological makeup. I read a lot of material from these authors and publishing houses trying to consume every bit of teaching I could on the topic. I wanted to "free" myself from a demonic force I thought was causing my mental health issues. I was wrong. The advice I took from these books not only increased my mental health problems, but it also made me refuse to seek treatment and also caused demonic oppression to actually happen in a way that was much worse than I could have ever imagined.

Some may find this claim strange, and since this is my experience, I do not want someone running to me or emailing me telling me their life stories that say these books are true. I cannot validate or refute your experiences, much like you cannot validate or refute mine.

That is always where the problem lies. When we rely on people's existential moments to define spiritual and/or biblical truths, we are accepting an extra-biblical source as a legitimate hermeneutic. This always leads to problems. The history of the church is filled with these kinds of issues. Just look at the Word-Faith and prosperity movements today, their claim to existential theology has made them set up "deliverance" offices where they will charge you money to relieve you of a demon "possession" that most likely you do not even have to begin with. In the process, because these Word-Faith charlatans are doing something unbiblically spiritual, this allows for the demonic to possibly act with God's judgment. If you are a true regenerate Christian, then God will decide whether to send demons to test you, correct you and even sanctify you from going through this nonsense again.

What is being presented in this book is a long study of the biblical passages that show directly how demonic creatures need to approach God before coming after people that are protected by the Holy Spirit. The idea that Satan has the ability to just walk up to a believing Christian and cause them problems because you stubbed your toe on a children's toy and spoke a curse word is not the way the Bible shows that kind of oppression to happen. Sin can lead to demonic problems. I cannot deny that. However, with the full context of the Bible to consider, even if we sin, it does not open a direct door to the demonic to oppress you. The sin you committed may cause demonic problems, but that is up to the triune-Godhead to decide. Not any demonic presence.

This is one reason I wrote this original paper for Seminary. I was tired of the amount of garbage "deliverance" books on the Christian market. None of them were claiming any biblical source for how these books claim demonic oppression/possession happens. To be honest, all the claims these books made are assumptions with no scriptural backing. I have seen these authors try to defend it, in the end the exegesis fails, and it shows more eisegesis and that these authors are reading their own experiences into the biblical account.

This book shows that there are four very distinct stories from the Bible that show just how demonic oppression happens. Many people will disagree and get angry with me saying that. However, there is no account of someone sinning and getting possessed because of that sin alone. There are accounts of Jesus healing someone that was afflicted because of sin, but that is no indicator that a demonic possession happened because of the sin giving power to that demon. The biblical accounts that will be exegeted will show that someone within the covenant community suffering with these issues is under testing and possibly judgment by God.

A few housekeeping issues need to be stated about the text that will soon open before you. First, you will notice that in direct Old Testament quotes, that whenever "Lord" or "LORD" comes up, I will use the typeset "LORD". Then in another place when talking about that reference I will simply type "Lord". All this is doing is quoting the text as directly as possible. Since I would like to respect the biblical text itself, and frankly the very name of God itself "Yahweh", when directly quoting an Old Testament passage that in the Hebrew mentions God's name, I have used a small caps "LORD".

Also, anyone reading this book that is from a secular, progressive theology or liberal theology, will see that I use BC and AD instead of BCE and CE. Again, this is a matter of respect for the biblical text. While you as the reader may feel that I am being disrespectful of the larger world and cultural diversity in the world, I am simply using a term for a time period that is respectful to my own personal beliefs and convictions.

Lastly, while I could have spent months, even years, expanding the issues that I use footnotes to say that I am using "x" definition in this issue, I wanted to keep the original manuscript as intact as possible. Some issues needed to be expanded and a few extra pages of explanation on a certain issue were written along with over a page of additional footnotes themselves. These issues were brought up because in the context of what this book is arguing, academically, the issue needs to be dealt with properly with what the thesis of this books' argument is.

Some of you may not like that I did not do similar with other issues. With those issues I would ask for you to consult the bibliography and extended recommended books for additional research on the topic. There is always a lot of reading to go through on an issue like this. If you are going to email me complaining about some claim I made in my book, all I ask is that you understand the argument and at least look over the source material I am using before doing so. I am not requiring you to agree with me in the slightest. In order for iron to sharpen iron, it sometimes takes two genuine regenerate Christians to sit down and talk about their disagreements. Calmly talking about disagreements is something that has been missing from a lot of open theology forums either in conference settings or online platforms.

If we walk away from such a discussion disagreeing, I have no problem with that. On the other hand, if someone comes after me for saying something they did not like and not having done the research to back up their claims or find out what exactly the research I have done is, it will not go well. If you have questions, please contact me at the email address provided in the first two pages of this book.

In the end, what I am hoping for is that you as a reader can appreciate more of what God has done, is doing and will do not just in your life but in the life of the entire church militant until Christ's return.

All the exegesis I have done I have tried in all ways to point it either back to Christ or to the triune-Godhead. If Christ through God is not magnified in what is being claimed here, then I am truly sorry.

Christ gave his life freely so that we could be free from the bonds of sin and know true life and salvation. When Christ did that and then rose from the grave, he claimed all those that he chose before the foundation of the world as his. It is like a seagull or child that reaches out and says "mine". This is a very weak analogy as Jesus is not going to caw like a bird or giggle like a child when claiming what is his. I believe that Jesus will look at any demonic force trying to steal away a lamb and that demon will run in fear from the Messiah shepherd that has claimed you and me for his own. The demonic simply have no claim on us in any way. Praise Jesus!

In order not to leave anyone hanging after the conclusion I have also included an article I wrote for my Substack, Reformed Demonology. This article will help anyone that finds themselves under demonic attack know what to do about the situation. The answer is not what most of those garbage "deliverance" books are saying. The quote from Michael in Jude 9, "The Lord rebuke you!" has many more connotations in the Greek than most of us would know or realize upon a surface reading of the present-day English. The original article is edited in the version of this book. Some things did need to be corrected.

I hope that you the reader in taking this material in will come to find comfort and reassurance in finding shelter with God. In the end, it is all about the triune-God wanting to redeem his creation for his glory. In doing so, he has naturally protected us from evil spiritual beings that must plead with God before even coming near us. These demons are too scared not to obey God's prohibition on them from approaching us directly.

Sola Scriptura!
Sola Fide!
Sola Gratia!
Solus Christus!
Soli Deo Gloria!

Anthony Uyl
- Author and Publisher

Chapter I - Introduction

To say there is a misunderstanding about demonology within the church would be an understatement. The reason such a statement can be made is that the direction of today's scholarship is moving away from the traditional roles or beliefs about the demonic in the world, the realms of heaven/hell and also the way it plays out in the church. What is interesting to note is that many Christians have enacted a policy of "see no evil, hear no evil, speak no evil" when it comes to instituting any theological position on the demonic in the world.

It is becoming more important. There are many books out on the Christian book market speaking of Spiritual Warfare (a branch of Christian demonology) and these books are being written primarily by charismatic and Pentecostal writers. When reading these texts, it is obvious there is no serious scholarship. The amount of eisegesis is evident as many of the claims these writers are making are in no way supported by scripture. Most of these charismatic books, if not all, are relying on their experiences when dealing with the demonic, rather than asking the question about what the Bible itself actually has to say about the forces of darkness.

Part of the reason for this could be the amounts of books on demonology, not just by secular authors, but also by many occultists through history. It is very easy to find texts even on Kindle, about ancient grimoires that list entire hosts of demon names. These names are derived from ancient sources the church has had no contact with for hundreds of years. With the prevalence of public domain books on the internet today, many Christian writers have started responding with kneejerk reaction books rather than delving into what the Bible has to say. Books such as *The Demon Dictionary Volumes I & II* by Kimberly Daniels, is a perfect example of this kneejerk action. Daniels' books are absolutely lacking in academic content and with barely any references to scripture. Ms. Daniels expects readers to accept her conclusions without referencing any evidence. Daniels expects that her experiences are good enough.

Too many people are relying on experiences to explain biblical demonology. This is in error. Jeremiah 17:9a explains that "The heart is deceitful above all things" (Jeremiah 17:9a ESV). This statement alone tells us that we should not be relying on what we feel or experience to define the demonic apart from scripture. Once someone starts to do that, problems will inherently arise.

Can anyone say that there are definite things about the demonic that can be taught from scripture? Anyone familiar with the Bible would answer in the affirmative. Yet still, in their readings, their exegesis and conclusions are formed by preconceived notions. Even some scholars will read an extra-biblical source and come to conclusions about the Bible that are simply not within the text itself and are completely absurd.

One thing we must realize is that the Old Testament is surprisingly lacking in demonology references. While I am no Hebrew scholar, from what I have read, the word "shed" or "sed" (שֵׁד šēḏ)[1] is the common Hebrew word used to describe the Old Testament understanding of what we call the demonic. But even these references that are referred to as "demons" are surprisingly lacking compared to the New Testament. While there are many other Hebrew references to demonic entities such as the "Tanin", "Leviathan", "Burning Serpents" or even the "Lilit", these references still do not make up an equal percentage of references to the demonic in the Old Testament as compared to the New.

So once again the question becomes, can the readers of the Bible, either the Old or New Testament, come to a definite demonology based on the lacking textual evidence? Again, the answer is yes! It only becomes a problem when "scholars" or writers try to define demonological truth outside of what the biblical testimony actually says. When looking at the text, there are readers who do not want to accept what the Bible has to say or come to the proper conclusions about what the text directly says. If any reader is able to remove their own bias about what the demonic is and how God has decided to deal with their kind in the grander scope of redemptive history, they will find that there is a rich tradition that has largely been ignored.

There are many things that can be said about the demonic within the testimony of the Bible. What is key to understand, is that the Bible is not about the workings of the spiritual world. While we cannot take the spiritual out of the Bible's redemptive history, there has to be a recognition that the Bible's intent is not to give us every answer about the domain of evil. The testimony of scripture is pointing to Christ, and the purpose of Christ in redeeming the world and sanctifying his church. What is ironic, is that the demonic in scripture are being shown as unwillingly assisting in this process. This may seem absurd, but the story of different texts shows that God is in control of exactly what Satan, or demons, are capable of in the world. So, the purpose of this book is to show this very sanctifying process. Yes, there is a demonic reality we must confront. Then there must be a definition of what the demonic is and how scripture shows that these forces of evil are being used by God to unwillingly sanctify the church. A thesis of this type is ridiculous to some. The accounts of the demonic in the Bible point to this very fact.

The first section will deal with the origins of demons. There is more than one theory that take this into consideration, some that have more credibility than others. Scholars argue for three possible origins, but there are many occultic and pagan sources that suggest other origins of demonic spirits. This section will primarily focus on the three biblical explanations. The three

---

1. Francis Brown, Samuel Rolles Driver, and Charles Augustus Briggs, *Enhanced Brown-Driver-Briggs Hebrew and English Lexicon* (Oxford, United Kingdom: Clarendon Press, 1977), 994.

suggestions of demonic origins are: 1) that the demonic are the souls of a pre-Adamic race that was destroyed between Genesis 1:1 and Genesis 1:2, 2) that the demonic are the souls of the Nephilim that were destroyed during the flood, and lastly 3) that the demonic are fallen angels that were thrown out of heaven with Satan's rebellion. All three of these theories will be considered with option 3 being considered most likely. An occult theory of the demonic will be considered. How this is important to the thesis will also be related here.

The second section will start an exegesis of Job 1:1-2:10, and chapter 42. The goal of this large section is to see how God (Yahweh) was in heaven when Satan showed up. While there are different views on what "the" Satan represents here, the exegesis will plainly show that the Satan referred to here is most likely the traditional Satan of church history. Once this is established, the analysis will continue to see how Satan challenged God about Job's righteousness, that Job's righteousness was shallow because of God's material blessings to Job. God allowed Satan to test Job twice to prove that Satan's accusation was right. By the end of Job 2:10 the exegesis will prove that Satan had failed. Satan will disappear in failure as Job defiantly refuses to "curse God and die." Even though his wife in this section of text tells Job to do this exact thing, Job still does not concede to the evil. Job remains righteous. With his righteousness proven, the exegesis will move to the end of Job in chapter 42. Here the analysis will show that though Job suffered at the hand of demonic powers, God will restore Job and bless him greatly for proving righteous.

For the next part of exegesis, an attempt to look at the text of Luke 22:31-34. In this section of Luke is where Jesus tells Peter that Satan has asked to sift all the apostles like wheat. The exegesis will focus on the person and work of Peter as after this proclamation by Christ, Peter fails to resist the devil by giving into the foreshadowing in v. 34 where Peter would disown Jesus three times. The analysis will also show that the warning about being sifted like wheat was not a point to say that Peter was not sanctified or "saved," but was at a moment of testing for the apostle. Unlike Job, the final blessing of Peter on the church, and the world, is not fully explained in the Bible. Some texts may hint at Peter's blessing, the texts of history show that Peter accomplished great things for the church right up until Peter being crucified upside down in Rome. There are a lot of assumptions about Peter and his founding of the Roman Catholic Church, but this discussion will be avoided to point to the direct blessing of Peter's faith.

A shift will be done to go back to the Old Testament to show that the demonic cannot just do testing of God's people any time they desire. To look at this properly, first an exegesis of 1 Kings 22:13-29 will be done. Within this text it once again shows God (Yahweh) sitting on the throne and desiring for a "spirit" to fill the mouths of the false prophets with lies. This can cause some moral problems for certain members within the church. At this moment, it is seen that this moment is a moment of testing both Ahab and Jehoshaphat in their war against the Arameans. Within this text is shown that a spirit of some kind, it will be assumed this is a demon, is sent to give lies to the two kings as a form of testing. By looking at this testing it will show that Ahab failed miserably in the test. This testing proved to be Ahab's downfall in the battle against the army of Aram. The test issued by God may seem opposite than the goal of sanctification. However, since Jehoshaphat also failed the test to listen to Micaiah, because of this the king of Judah failed in the sanctification that God was using the test to perform.

For a final exegetical analysis, the text in Zechariah 3 will be considered. The point of this part of the exegesis is to show that there are times when God (Yahweh) plainly says, no. Satan here wanted to accuse the high priest, Joshua, but the angel of the Lord commanded that Satan be rebuked for wanting to move against Joshua. While the exact identity of the angel of Yahweh will not be given consideration in the exegesis, the rebuke that limits Satan from bringing accusations and testing against a person in God's covenant people is the focus. While in all the other texts that have been analyzed, there is an effort to show that God is the one that allows demons to test his people, in this case, God stops it before it begins. Many times, Christians in the church will assume that Satan can attack or oppress Christians without any limitations. The text shows that God has limits that cannot be crossed. Although Satan needs God's permission to test and afflict the believing community, Satan is not always given permission from God.

A final consideration will be given to the testing of the church over the course of church history. There is an assumed argument that will be made about the persecutions of the church committed by empires such as Rome, the Islamic states, or even Protestants during the Reformation. This assumption is that there was an evil spiritual force behind it. While the documents of history will never confirm such an association, it is a fair one to make. Regardless of the source of the persecutions, the fact is that the church rose out of a dangerous situation to become more holy and more predominant in the world. Each time that a government or other social force has attempted to dismantle the church, it has only made the believing community become bigger and more sanctified. Many of these times of persecution ended with great men of faith that were able to show a way of holiness that was not considered during the time of persecution. To ignore the benefits that happened during these trying times is ignorant. God used the hard times, influenced by evil spiritual forces, to grow and sanctify his people.

Chapter II - Origins of the Demonic

The origins of the spirits known as demons has been something that many scholars within and outside the Christian community have struggled with for many years. As was mentioned in the introduction, the Bibles purpose is not to give us all the details about where the angelic and demonic forces come from. The angels and demons simply are not the focus of the biblical story. Christ is the centre. The rest of the Bible rotates around the coming, the death and resurrection and eventual return of the Messiah King.

Although this is the Bibles focus, there is enough textual evidence to point to where the demonic come from. These considerations will give weight to the argument of the thesis. If the demonic are the result of anything but fallen angels, then the submission they endure cannot make sense biblically. There is a lot of disagreement over the issue over human freewill and determinism, if demons were once mortal, then it only reasons that they too have the same amount of freewill as a human being. The Bible does not seem to afford demons that luxury.

The first theory of demonic origins that will be presented is also the most unlikely. The idea of the "gap theory," that there was a period of time between Genesis 1:1 and 1:2 has fallen out of common usage today. This is not to say that there are absolutely no people that believe it to be true. There are some scholars and laypeople that firmly believe the gap theory to be a reality. Unfortunately, the biblical evidence for such thinking is severely lacking.

Demonologists are also in this camp when it comes to demonic origins. Some Christian, and occult, demonologists have a strong belief that the demons the world deals with today are the products of a pre-Adamic race.[1] This pre-Adamic race was eliminated by God. This widescale destruction is believed to have been caused by Satan.[2] It was during this pre-Adamic rebellion that Satan was cast out from Heaven. As a result of this destruction, the souls of the pre-Adamic race became the demons that exist today.[3]

The question must be asked: is the gap theory tenable? At first thought a theologian might think it is ridiculous, but at the same time it may not be completely so.

> [Some] believe that there may be a "gap" or, better, a lapse of time be-fore the six, twenty-four hours days of Genesis begin. In this case, the first verse of the Bible would not necessarily indicate the

---

1. Leonard Thompson, *Demons* (Joplin, Missouri: College Press Publishing Company, 2005), 42.
2. Thompson, *Demons*, 42.
3. Thompson, *Demons*, 42.

original ex nihilo creation of God, but more recent acts of God forming a world He had previously created.[4]

Another line of argument lies within the concept of darkness. Within this argument is the idea that the Hebrew words that are used to say, "without form and void" and also "darkness" in Genesis 1:2 is a reflection of a post-apocalyptic act of God.[5] While it may be hard to directly pull that from the biblical text some textual critics have pointed that way. Since they have, attempts by other scholars have been made to refute the claims. Those refutations have been successful. At the same time: from a theoretical standpoint, this would seem to make a lot of sense. The idea of judgment from God is often associated with the idea of darkness within the text of the Old Testament.

Taking the argument further, demonologists that agree with this creation method will use the texts in Isaiah 14:12ff. and Ezekiel 28:1-9 as evidence that Satan's fall was pre-Adamic.[6] There is a large problem with this assumption. These texts have classically been interpreted as describing Satan and why he fell from heaven. This is probably not a correct correlation of the texts. Within the context of each set of verses, it is clearly talking about a foreign king whose pride is such of that of some celestial being. Isaiah 14:12ff. is clearly speaking of the king of Babylon at the time. Ezekiel 28:1-9 is speaking of the king of Tyre. Granted, it is clear that there is some kind of ancient Israelite archetype being used here. To automatically attribute that to Satan is a large stretch of the text. While the text may seem to be speaking of the traditional fall of Satan and his host, when these texts are kept in context, these texts may not be speaking of that reality in any way. To further drive home the point, even if these texts are talking about the fall of Satan, the texts themselves do not point to this happening in a pre-Adamic time. There simply is no link to such a distinction.

Many people inside and outside the church are easily swayed by such stories as they fancifully think of what a pre-Adamic race could look like. Also, the thinking of what kind of spirituality they had themselves may fill the minds of present-day people. While these fantastical dreams may fill imaginations with grand ideas, there needs to be a grounding. Thinking of things that are theories and dreaming of possibilities that may not be possible is always a dangerous thing to do. What needs to be considered is the biblical evidence. Does the Bible say or suggest that such a pre-Adamic time existed? Most likely it does not. The evidence seems to be a point of eisegesis rather than exegesis.

This gap theory has many problems that simply cannot be ignored. This biggest criticism is that there is no evidence in scripture that explicitly states there was another "creation" before our own.[7] If there is no biblical evidence

---

4. Norman Geisler, *Systematic Theology, Volume Two* (Minneapolis, Minnesota: Bethany House, 2003), 645.

5. Wayne Grudem, *Systematic Theology*, (Grand Rapids, Michigan: Zondervan, 1994), 287.

6. Thompson, *Demons*, 42.

7. Grudem, *Systematic Theology*, 288.

of such an event, then readers must be very skeptical that such a theory is possible. The definition of "darkness" implying "judgment" on the surface may seem plausible, but there is also a contextual issue as there are times in the Old Testament when darkness simply means, it was dark out. What is also of note is that at the end of the creation account God calls it "good" and then shortly after "very good" (Genesis 1:31). To indicate that God had created something good, and then destroyed it would imply that God had ultimately failed to redeem his own creation. The redemptive-historical arch of scripture would suggest otherwise in this "second" creation. Unless a gap theorist tries to say that God was making a "test run" this cannot be. Even if God was making a test run, there once again indicates that God can still fail. A God that can fail at any level is a God that is powerless to save.

If the gap theory is untenable biblically, then so is the thinking that demons are disembodied souls of the pre-Adamic race. The whole thought of disembodied spirits is mere speculation at best.[8] While historically, there has been a belief within pagan thought that the dead could become demons, there is no evidence biblically of this. Interestingly, there are ancient texts that suggest a demon can be the spirit/soul of a dead human.[9] Since there is no way to prove that there was a pre-Adamic race, this conclusion about ancient paganism, specifically Greco beliefs, are not appropriate in this context. This may be a historical point of spiritual and/or pagan beliefs, but in this case, it cannot be used. The dead becoming demons has long been a belief in pagan belief structures, but there is more to it than most Christian scholars want to recognize. Since the idea of the gap theory is unsupported speculation, the pre-Adamic dead simply cannot be the demonic beings that exist in the world today.

A second theory that is once again finding traction in modern scholarship is the idea that the demonic are the souls of the Nephilim destroyed in the flood.[10] There are often statements that the Jews of the first-century believed that the story of the giants and Nephilim in Genesis 6 was the explanation for the origin of the demonic.[11] Heiser acknowledges that this may be an interpretive leap for modern readers, but he tries to further explain that this was not the case for the Second Temple Jew. These were the texts they had been exposed to for generations. Since this is what the early Jewish readers had,[12] Jesus had to work with it in explaining the demonic. Same with New Testa-

---

8. Thompson, *Demons*, 42.

9. J. E. Rexine, "Daimōn in Classical Greek Literature," *Greek Orthodox Theological Review* 30.3 (1985): 335–61.

10. Like many issues surrounding demons and Satan in this paper, this is simply a bigger issue than can appropriately be presented here. While I and Heiser both agree that the Nephilim are the children of a human and angel/demonic union, the debate rages on today. There are many arguments that can be made for the three theories, but the ones I find most convincing are that the Nephilim are sired by angels/demons. This does not mean that I agree with Heiser's arguments about the demonic origins from Nephilim souls.

11. Michael S. Heiser, *Demons: What the Bible Really Says about the Powers of Darkness* (Bellingham, Washington: Lexham Press, 2020), 127.

12. Heiser, *"Demons"*, 128.

ment authors. Heiser makes the claim that New Testament authors assumed these beliefs into their own demonology within the New Testament.

The argument's origin is then made clear. The writings of 1 Enoch and Jubilees emerged from the Second Temple Period. Heiser claims that these texts were more important than we think they were. Since these texts were supposedly so important to Second Temple Jews, later New Testament writers assumed the beliefs in 1 Enoch into their theology.[13] 1 Enoch is noted as saying that,

> Evil spirits have proceeded from their bodies [human women]; because they are born from men, and from the holy Watchers is their beginning and primal origin; they shall be evil spirits on earth, and evil spirits shall they be called. As for the spirits of heaven [the angelic host], in heaven shall be their dwelling, but as for the spirits of the earth which were born upon the earth, on the earth shall be their dwelling. And the spirits of the giants afflict, oppress, destroy, attack, do battle, and work destruction on the earth, and cause trouble: they take no food, but nevertheless hunger and thirst, and cause offences. And these spirits shall rise up against the children of men and against the women, because they have proceeded from them.[14]

The idea of this thinking has been established for a long time. Even the Greeks, as mentioned above, believed that the dead could become demons. There is a precedent set forth for this.

The fallacy with this argument, and Heiser's belief in general, is the exaltation of the Second Temple Judaic writings. While, yes, it is important to keep context in mind. It is also important to remember that not everything written in the ancient world was truthful. Some of it, could have been fiction, or a story, without any serious consideration for truth. The modern reader and Bible student can attest that Jude might directly quote 1 Enoch, and 2 Peter 2 may allude to Enoch, but that does not mean that 1 Enoch and/or Jubilees are legitimate sources of truth. Paul quotes from pagan philosophers to make some points, but it does not make the pagan philosopher's writings true in their entirety. While someone like Heiser would deny they are performing this accusation: it appears that these translators are elevating canonically uninspired texts to the same level as canonically inspired ones. The assumption alone that 1 Enoch and Jubilees were accepted as general truth by the first century Jews is largely an assumption that is not true. Heiser needs to believe this in order for his argument to be plausible.

To further explain this argument, what many claim about 1 Enoch is also a claim in ignorance. I have personally been involved in online arguments with some that defend the accuracy of 1 Enoch because it was found in the Dead Sea Scrolls. What is important to remember here is that only fractions

---

13. Heiser, "*Demons*", 144.

14. 1 Enoch 15:9-11. R. H. Charles (translator), *The Book of Enoch Revised* (Ingersoll, Ontario: Devoted Publishing, 2019), 26.

of 1 Enoch were found in the caves at Qumran. 1 Enoch has a long nearly two-thousand-year history outside of the caves at Qumran. Biblical scholarship has shown that while 1 Enoch was initially started in its writing approximately 300 BC, the completion of 1 Enoch happened sometime in the early pre-Christian era.[15] What this essentially means is that 1 Enoch was completed after the closing of the New Testament canon.

This opens up an entire world of possibilities about where these quotes in Jude and references in 2 Peter 2 come from. Since we cannot affirm with absolute surety that the quotes in the Bible are from a confirmed completed 1 Enoch manuscript, we have to take that argument into critique. It is possible. To say it is not would be a plea to ignorant assumption. However, since the text was not completed at this time, it is highly possible the Jude quote and 2 Peter 2 reference came from another Second Temple text that is now lost by God's providence. Since this is a likelihood, we all must be careful in taking the argument that the 1 Enoch book was found in the Dead Seas Scrolls as one hundred percent verification of this claim. One professor of mine in Seminary commented that it is also possible that some of the caves in Qumran were garbage caves. Since papyri in those days was so valuable, a text of false information could not just be thrown away. The papyri could be used for other purposes. While there is nothing to verify a claim like this, as I said above, we have to be careful in assuming that every ancient text we have is true or an accurate account of what we need it to be. This is the case with 1 Enoch.

There is also an assumption that every Nephilim was evil. Heiser once again makes the claim that the Nephilim "subrace" was evil to a different degree of humanity. Heiser claims this based off the fact that the Nephilim were bred from divine beings. Since these divine beings were not followers of God (Yahweh), God in a way discarded them. Since God had no use for the Nephilim, Yahweh was compelled to wipe the assumingly "evil" subrace of humanity from the earth.[16] The Bible itself never says that the Nephilim race was evil in its entirety. There could have been a time when a Nephilim was righteous. Since Heiser makes many speculative claims about the Nephilim, then so can anyone else. If Nephilim could possibly be righteous, why are they all demons? Why not angels? "Metatron [Enoch] explains how and why he was taken up and reveals in detail the steps by which he was transformed in mind and body from a human being into an angel."[17] If Enoch himself was made into an angel, then so could a Nephilim. The assumption always seems to be that the dead are made into the demonic. What needs to be realized is that the demonic in Greco religion was neutral and not always evil.

---

15. E. Isaac, "1 (Ethiopic Apocalypse of) Enoch (Second Century B.C.–First Century A.D.) A New Translation and Introduction" in *The Old Testament Pseudepigrapha, Volume 1*, ed. James H. Charlesworth (New York; New York: Yale University Press, 1983), 7.

16. Michael S. Heiser, *The Unseen Realm: Recovering the Supernatural Worldview of the Bible, First Edition.* (Bellingham, Washington: Lexham Press, 2015), 203.

17. F. I. Anderson, "2 (Hebrew Apocalypse of) Enoch (Late First Century A.D.) Appendix: 2 Enoch in Merilo Pravednoe, A New Translation and Introduction" in *The Old Testament Pseudepigrapha, vol. 1*, ed. James H. Charlesworth (New York, New York: Yale University Press, 1983), 223.

While theologically, it can be made that they are evil, in the context of the ancient Greek religion, they were not.

In the last couple decades, there are two other writers that have been making waves as far as the Nephilim argument goes. Both of these writers are defenders of the idea that the souls of the Nephilim are the spirits we now call demons.

The first of these authors is a man by the name of Derek P. Gilbert. Gilbert's book *The Second Coming of Saturn* highly relies on the arguments that Heiser makes in his own books. This book revolves around the idea that the "watchers" from 1 Enoch descended on Mount Hermon,[18] much as Heiser argues, and created the Nephilim. The problem is that this claim about Mount Hermon is not supported biblically. Gilbert tries to make an argument for it, but it simply does not stand up. Hermon is never mentioned as a descending place for the demonic, no specific place is within the context of the entire biblical canon. All Revelation 12 states is that the rebellious angels were thrown out of heaven. This reference to Mount Hermon as the place that the "watchers" descended is simply a forcing of an unbiblical text, 1 Enoch, into the biblical accounts. There are many other areas that Mount Hermon is forced into the biblical accounts with absolutely no textual credibility. Despite Gilbert's claims, it is all speculation and nothing more.

As an additional note, the term "watcher" is used in the Daniel 4 ESV translation. This does appear to be a reference not to an evil angel, but one that Yahweh sends. The idea of the watchers being evil spirits is again something that 1 Enoch is being used to force into the canonical biblical text.

The second of these authors is someone by the name of Ryan Pitterson. Thankfully, Pitterson does something that both Heiser and Gilbert fail to do. Pitterson rightfully calls out 1 Enoch for being, not just a non-biblical text, but a heretical one. In Chapter 12: Are "Extra-Biblical" Texts Really Biblical? in Pitterson's book *Judgments of the Nephilim*,[19] he makes several accurate claims about the legitimacy of the book of 1 Enoch. While the examples are many in that chapter, I will highlight two that are showing the heretical nature of the account of 1 Enoch.

The first text of 1 Enoch that Pitterson points out is 1 Enoch 9:1-3,

> And then Michael, Uriel, Raphael, and Gabriel looked down from heaven and saw much blood being shed upon the earth, and all lawlessness being wrought upon the earth. And they said one to another: "The earth made without inhabitant cries the voice of their crying up to the gates of heaven. And now to you, the holy ones of heaven, the souls of men make their suit, saying, 'Bring our cause before the Most High.'"[20]

---

18. Derek P. Gilbert, *The Second Coming of Saturn: The Great Conjunction, America's Temple, and the Return of the Watchers* (Crane, Missouri: Defender, 2021), 21.

19. Ryan Pitterson, *Judgment of the Nephilim* (New York, New York: Days of Noe Publishing, 2017), 209-241.

20. Charles, *Enoch*, 21.

It is kind of surprising that such a problematic text has to be explained. In online discussions about 1 Enoch, some have tried to argue with me that prayer to angels is not "worship". The Bible is clear that prayer alone belongs to God. In Matthew 6:9, the famous start to the "Lord's Prayer" Jesus commands to "pray like this: Our Father who art in heaven." This is not a defence to say that we can pray to angels, saints or Mary. Jesus is commanding us that when we pray, to pray to God alone. Prayer to another spiritual being is a form of worship. You are ascribing worth or spiritual intercessory power to a being other than God that has none. If someone argues that prayer to angels and/or saints is not worship or sinful, then the door opens to those in occultic or other practices that pray to what Christian's would define as demons. If these practitioners are not "worshipping" the demon by praying to it, then there is no foul. This is a ridiculous claim to make. However, the door does open for someone to make such a boast if the unbiblical prayer to angels is justified. Since the words of Jesus in Matthew 6 strictly show to pray to God alone, prayer to anything but God is heresy.

The second text out of 1 Enoch is even more problematic. That is 1 Enoch 100:10-13

> And now, know ye *that from the angels He will inquire as to your deeds in heaven, from the sun and from the moon and from the stars in reference to your sins because upon the earth ye execute judgement on the righteous.* And He will summon to testify against you every cloud and mist and dew and rain; for they shall all be withheld because of you from descending upon you, and they shall be mindful of your sins. *And now give presents to the rain that it be not withheld from descending upon you, nor yet the dew, when it has received gold and silver from you that it may descend.* When the hoar-frost and snow with their chilliness, and all the snow-storms with all their plagues fall upon you, in those days ye shall not be able to stand before them.[21] (italics added)

I would honestly hope that such a text would be self-explainable. Unfortunately, many will claim that it is not. God will call the angels to go ask the natural forces of this world if humanity was good to it. So, Enoch, tells his readers to go and offer "presents" to forces like the rain. This is flat-out pagan practice. To put it another way, this is occultic witchcraft. It is not biblical in any way. The Bible affirms in Deuteronomy 18:9-14 that these things are an "abomination" and that those that practice them are to be cast out from the community, even put to death. The heretical nature of such a passage need not be explained much further. I would hope that all readers will see this for what it is.

Christians are always warned throughout their lives that the way the enemy deceives us is to mix in a nugget of truth and slowly pull that person away from the truth. 1 Enoch does exactly that. Exposing just these two pass-

---

21. Charles, *Enoch*, 91.

ages shows that: 1) 1 Enoch is not a biblical text, 2) 1 Enoch is not to be used to verify something the Bible does not speak to, nor directly support, and 3) in the end, 1 Enoch is a distinctly anti-Christian text. If these heretical verses were not in 1 Enoch, I would not make the third statement. Since those passages are, 1 Enoch is an anti-Christ text. The truth of 1 Enoch cannot be stated any other way.[22]

Unfortunately, Pitterson does not stop there. After proving that 1 Enoch is a heretical and anti-Christian text, Pitterson then in Chapter 21: Demons - Spirits of the Dead Nephilim, turns around and uses 1 Enoch to say that the spirits of the dead Nephilim are possibly demons. What is strange, in Chapter 12 where Pitterson rebukes 1 Enoch his references to the book are mentioning it as "pseudo-Enoch" (the pseudo prefix comes from the Greek work ψευής [pseuēs] meaning "lying" or "false") yet in Chapter 21 he names the book by its proper name "1 Enoch". This is an odd change to make. Pitterson then wants to turn to the Bible to see if such a claim is true.[23]

Pitterson's first point of proof is to say that angels (malak/angelos) have bodies and that demons do not. The proof texts used are Genesis 18, 19, Daniel 9, Jude and Hebrew 13:2. Genesis 18 and 19 speak of angels, and Yahweh, coming to visit Abraham to speak with Abraham about Sodom. Pitterson makes the claim that the angels in that instance, because they appeared as men, have literal physical bodies. As well, in Daniel 9 the angel Gabriel comes and touches Daniel which to Pitterson indicates the reality of a true physical body. The same implication is made about Hebrews 13:2 because the angels physically visit people in secret so must have bodies. Next, in Jude

---

22. Although I hesitate to bring it up, some might ask the question about the Book of Jasher. Like with the book of 1 Enoch, only one reference text is needed to show the problems with the Book of Jasher: "And Joseph reached his mother's grave, and Joseph hastened and ran to his mother's grave, and fell upon the grave and wept. And Joseph cried aloud upon his mother's grave, and he said, O my mother, my mother, O thou who didst give me birth, awake now, and rise and see thy son, how he has been sold for a slave, and no one to pity him. O rise and see thy son, weep with me on account of my troubles, and see the heart of my brethren. Arouse my mother, arouse, awake from thy sleep for me, and direct thy battles against my brethren. O how have they stripped me of my coat, and sold me already twice for a slave, and separated me from my father, and there is no one to pity me. Arouse and lay thy cause against them before God, and see whom God will justify in the judgment, and whom he will condemn. Rise, O my mother, rise, awake from thy sleep and see my father how his soul is with me this day, and comfort him and ease his heart. And Joseph continued to speak these words, and Joseph cried aloud and wept bitterly upon his mother's grave; and he ceased speaking, and from bitterness of heart he became still as a stone upon the grave. And Joseph heard a voice speaking to him from beneath the ground, which answered him with bitterness of heart, and with a voice of weeping and praying in these words: *My son, my son Joseph, I have heard the voice of thy weeping and the voice of thy lamentation; I have seen thy tears; I know thy troubles, my son, and it grieves me for thy sake, and abundant grief is added to my grief. Now therefore my son, Joseph my son, hope to the Lord, and wait for him and do not fear, for the Lord is with thee, he will deliver thee from all trouble. Rise my son, go down unto Egypt with thy masters, and do not fear, for the Lord is with thee, my son.* And she continued to speak like unto these words unto Joseph, and she was still." (Book of Jasher 42:30-40) (italics added). What should be seen here is that the Book of Jasher supports the acts of necromancy. This is not biblical. The Bible condemns necromancy, spiritism or mediums on several occasions. Jasher, like 1 Enoch, is an anti-Christ text. Anthony Uyl (editor), *The Book of Jasher* (Woodstock, Ontario: Devoted Publishing, 2107), 125-126.

23. Pitterson, *Nephilim*, 415-416.

it speaks of angels being tormented and bound with chains, apparently, to Pitterson, this again confirms to him that angels have bodies since chains have to be used to contain them. Metaphorical anthropomorphism seems to be left out of this discussion. In Exodus 33:20-23, God (Yahweh) speaks to Moses that God will place Moses in the cleft of a rock where God will place his "hand" over Moses so that the glory of God's "face" will pass by, and Moses will be allowed to see God's "back". Since these terms are being used, then Yahweh must have a physical body. However, in John 4:24a Jesus tells the disciples that God is spirit. So, what is happening with Moses? God has allowed Moses to see him in an anthropomorphic way so that Moses can understand God. It does not mean that God has or had a body. Same with the angels. Just because they take on physical characteristics to interact with humans, does not mean that they definitely have a physical body. If that were true, then so would all of the Godhead and the Bible would contradict itself. There are other examples where in heaven Jesus is seen as a lamb (Revelation 5) again, this does not mean that Jesus' human body was transformed into a lamb when he ascended to the throne. It is an anthropomorphism that helps John (in that case) and the reader to understand what God is trying to say to us.

The rest of the arguments in the chapter rest on demons being spirits and angels not. Again, since this is a misunderstanding of hermeneutics, the arguments fall empty. Another claim is that demons as spirits cannot pass bodies of water according to Luke 11:24-26.[24] I am not sure how Pitterson is reading that into the text. All it says is the demon was sent to "waterless" places. Not that the demon as a spirit was incapable of crossing bodies of water. I do know where that thinking biblically comes from as it comes from ancient occultic thought[25] and not the Bible.

Another point of argument from some is that some of the ancient church fathers also believed that the demons were the souls of the dead Nephilim. I hinted at this critique earlier of ancient texts. Many times, in our present-day world, an ancient text is found, and scholars go over it trying to find what new information can be discovered. This information is often taken as nonfiction. I am not saying the writings of the early church fathers were fiction. Just that we often make immediate assumptions about ancient texts that we should not. This one I am suggesting here is: not all the church fathers were one hundred percent correct in their theology. The accusation that they were closer to the apostles than any of us may seem to be legitimate. I would even support that due to their cultural oral tradition, that the stories they heard were very likely accurate. Accurate does not mean true. Accurate could mean that it was something the apostle said. With the wealth of information and books we have in today's world, it is hard to see the evangelical church falling to

---

24. Pitterson, *Nephilim*, 417.
25. Elyze Zomer, "Demons and Tutelary Deities from Heaven", in *Was vom Himmel kommt*, ed. Gosta Gabirl, Brit Karger, Annette Zgoll and Christian Zgoll (Berlin, Germany: DeGruyter, 2021), 162, 164, 168. These texts show the use of water in repelling not only demonic spirits, but unwanted rodents and critters considered dangerous. All of these rituals use water to do so.

leftist theology, Word-Faith heresies, and other teachings that we have enough at the click of a mouse to disprove. If we, with as much verifiable information we have, cannot in even a decade maintain our composure for God's truth alone, how could we expect men who lived thousands of years ago to be able to affirm the truth of a statement since none of the people that the Bible claims were alive to confirm them are now dead? Also, there are many theological perspectives from early church fathers that many churches, even those using the early church fathers for evidence, would reject. John of Damascus was the father of Eastern Orthodoxy. No Protestant or even a Roman Catholic would be one hundred precept affirming what John of Damascus said. To get an Arminian to affirm Augustine would be a miracle from God alone! We have to be careful pulling evidence from the early church fathers as credible when the worldwide church cannot even verify as a whole, what is credible. We need other sources. The only source we should be going to is the Bible.

The historical origin of the demonic has been under attack in recent years. While the two theories explained above have been around throughout the his-tory of the church, there are more modern explanations than the ones that have been generally accepted in the evangelical church. While some scholars such as Heiser, question the biblical evidence that suggests that demons are fallen angels, the evidence that has already been shown points that scholars like Heiser are depending too heavily on Second Temple texts to prove their point. The biblical record, which is the unerring word of God, seems to suggest that the classical understanding of the demonic origins is the most palatable.

One proof text that is often disputed but at the same time describes the fall of the demonic host from heaven is Revelation 12:7-10. The context is often what is debated here saying that is more of a description of Israel and the church than of an actual heavenly event.[26] Yet, at the same time "An immediate consequence of the defeat of the devil and his hosts is that 'a place was not found for them any longer in heaven'."[27] For Satan and his host to have been thrown out of heaven, at some point they had to have been angels of heaven.

Jude 6 is another point of emphasis for the sin of the angels committed in having sexual relations with humans in Genesis 6. This verse is in debate about what it exactly says about the origin of the demonic, but from what it seems to say, "[a]nd the angels who did not stay within their own position of authority, but left their proper dwelling, he has kept in eternal chains under gloomy darkness until the judgment of the great day" (Jude 6 ESV). The verse does seem to indicate a punishment for angels that left their place of authority. A valid de-scription of the punishment for sin rather than the nature of the sin itself is given. Jude himself uses original Koine Greek to show that God is showing vengeance for some wrong committed by the fallen angels. The ang-

---

26. G. K. Beale, *The Book of Revelation: A Commentary on the Greek Text*, New International Greek Testament Commentary (Grand Rapids, Michigan: W.B. Eerdmans, 1999), 651.

27. Beale, *Revelation*, 655.

els did not keep their proper place, so God has "kept" them in "chains" and in "gloomy darkness". God will show judgment and vengeance against those that violate his righteous standards. These fallen angels cannot escape God's wrath in the place they have been sent to be bound.[28] The indication in this verse is that holy angels committed an act of sin and were cast out of heaven for it. Not only were these now fallen angels cast out, but they were bound in chains until a time of judgment.[29]

In order to argue against this view, scholars from the other two views of demonic origins have to accept authority from extra-biblical literature. In doing so, these scholars are accepting a source of biblical authority that were never accepted by everyone as inspired. The discussion about the inspired nature of 1 Enoch continues to this day, and while someone like Heiser may not directly say that 1 Enoch is inspired, he treats it like it is. Loren Stuckenbruck, who is quoted ad nauseum by Heiser, argues the same point. But the Second Temple texts cannot be argued for this kind of validity. These texts can be useful in understanding the cultural landscape of Palenstine at the time of Christ, they cannot be used to define biblical truth. The same falls for the gap theory. There are no texts that can confirm such a theory within the inspired biblical books themselves. If in these two theories, there is not enough biblical evidence to prove that either is completely true, then the texts must be questioned. The fallen angel's theory seems to be argued with certainty. To take other theories that are not supported in any kind of way is strange. Reading outside texts into the biblical accounts is more an act of eisegesis than exegesis.

What a scholar must not do when considering the origins of demons is to completely disregard the origins of the demonic from other ancient cultures. The Greek explanation has already been pointed out. Another common belief among ancient pagan nations in the ancient near east was the idea that demons were "born" by spiritual sexual union between different demons.

One of the earliest accounts we have of demons being sired by other demons is in a document known as *The Alphabet of Sirach*.[30] The text quotes the mother of demons as Lilith[31] the apparent first wife of Adam, "She also

---

28. Thomas R. Schreiner, *1, 2 Peter, Jude, vol. 37, The New American Commentary* (Nashville, Tennessee: Broadman & Holman Publishers, 2003), 448.

29. There are ancient, and modern, commentators that try to attribute the texts of Isaiah 14:12-21 to explain the ultimate fall of Satan as being about pride towards desiring God's position of authority. While that can be a plausible explanation, this specific passage in Isaiah, kept in context, is referring to a king of Babylon. When the history of Babylonian kings is studied, it is not hard to see that they indeed believed themselves to be in the place of God. A familiar ancient Hebrew archetype may be used here, but to say it directly describes Satan's fall is unlikely. Ezekiel 28:1-19 is categorized in a similar way. It is probably talking about some celestial event, but without further evidence, the context is talking about the Prince and King of Tyre. Again, like Isaiah, an ancient Hebrew archetype of some celestial event could be being used here, it is most likely not speaking of Satan directly.

30. The Alphabet of Sirach, also known as The Alphabet of Ben Sira, is supposedly written by the same person as the apocryphal book of "Wisdom of Sirach."

31. There is a lot of controversy over the person and demon of Lilith. While the idea that she was Adam's first wife is clearly speculative and unprovable, the fact that demons known as lilitu were a very real thing in the ancient near east. Even the text of Isaiah 34:14 where it is com-

agreed to have one hundred of her children die every day. Accordingly, every day one hundred demons."[32] The same document indicates that the demon Sammael, who is thought to be Satan,[33] as the father of the demon children. A second reference to the mother of demons being Lilith is also found in ancient bowls excavated from the area of the Tigris-Euphrates.[34]

The name Lilith may not be directly associated with the idea of sexual intercourse to make new demons, still the idea still exists in medieval and modern day occultic texts. A book written in the Middle Ages that was written to explain the claimed sexual interaction between witches and demons assumed that particular children in the world were born from demonic incubation.

> Now, it is undoubted by Theologians and philosophers that carnal intercourse between mankind and the Demon sometimes gives birth to human beings; that is how is to be born the Antichrist, according to some Doctors, such as Bellarmin, Suarez, Maluenda.[35]

Likewise, in an encyclopedia on occult spirits, the writer Judika Illes says that new spirits are born every day and that some humans have the ability to turn into spirits, or demons, after death. This depends on the spiritual traditions the person adheres to.[36] Illes indicates two different occultic demon origins, the support of the occultic belief in demonic progeny, or the dead possibly becoming demons is believed here as well.

The different origins of the demonic have been observed and assessed. The most likely and believable origin of the demonic host is that they are fallen angels, thrown out of heaven when they sinned. That sin is directly unknown, but the Bible indicates that the demons did in fact commit some sin. The occult origins of the demonic, while supported by pagan and cultural

---

monly interpreted as "screech owl" the word here indicates a lilitu type "creature." Since the lilitu is a demon of Assyrian origin, it is interesting that Isaiah, who was writing when the Assyrian empire was the dominating power of that day, mentions a lilitu in this passage. Older translations of Isaiah name the creature as "Lilith" but since lilitu's were more commonly a type of demon rather than a named one, it could be possible that Isaiah was referring to a type of demon that resides in the ruins of Edom. To read about the historical lilitu refer to: Rosemary Ellen Guiley, *The Encyclopedia of Demons & Demonology* (New York, New York: Checkmark Books, 2009), 147.

32. Wikipedia, *Alphabet of Sirach*, (Wikipedia, last updated October 23, 2021), https://en.wikipedia.org/wiki/Alphabet_of_Sirach. While I would not normally support using Wikipedia for scholarly research, this is the easiest version of the Alphabet of Sirach for readers to access.

33. Directly the thinking is that Sammael (Samael) was the serpent that tempted Eve. For further reading refer to: Rosemary Ellen Guiley, *The Encyclopedia of Demons & Demonology* (New York, New York: Checkmark Books, 2009), 221-222.

34. Jan Fries, *The Seven Names of Lamastu: A Journey through Mesopotamian Magick and Beyond* (London, England: Avalonia, 2016), 390. Also, within this book, on the same page is the name Naamah, a sister of Lilith, who also bears demonic children.

35. Sinistrari of Ameno, *Demoniality: Incubi and Succubi*, (loc. 249), Mockingbird Press LLC, Kindle.

36. Judika Illes, *Encyclopedia of Spirits: The Ultimate Guide to the Magic of Fairies, Genies, Demons, Ghosts, Gods & Goddesses* (New York, New York: HarperCollins, 2009), 19.

thought, is just as provable from the Bible to be not true. Many from occultic and pagan beliefs in the present day may dispute this fact, but the biblical evidence points elsewhere.

In the grand scheme of the thesis, does it matter? In fact, it does. If demons were originated from anything other than a direct creation and expulsion of God from heaven, then different, possibly human, attributes would be present. As well, humans are the ones who are said to be created in the image of God. Demons, and even angels, cannot claim this. If they could, then there would be more ability for demons to repent and also to have more individual freedoms than the Bible suggests that they do. If demons were once human, born with God's image, then the text in Job 1&2 that they could only test Job with God's permission will fail.

At its core, there is a much more dangerous implication with the idea that mortal souls could become demons. When observing occultic belief, specifically within the tradition known as hermeticism, a form of occultism that arose out of Judeo-Christianity, the idea of the demonic is nearly equal to the idea of what we as Christians would define as a god or gods. These occultists would deny such a claim simply because of how their belief in "God" works.

These practicing occultists all believe that we are infused with what the Manichaeans defined as a piece of the Kingdom of Light that is attempting to be reunited with the great god of the Manichaean belief.[37] This is also the central teaching of hermeticism. That "God" is in all and part of all. That since "God" is part of us and yet transcendent that the greatest manifestation of "God" is ourselves and our search to once again be reunited with "God".[38] The hermetic occultists will affirm that there is something divine in us, much like with the Nephilim. In essence, the occultic practitioners of today are calling all humans Nephilim.

The importance of this cannot be overstated. Simply because within the hermetic traditions there is a belief in two "paths". The first the Right-Hand Path. While the ultimate goals and ideologies of the two are unimportant for this study the Right-Hand Path believes that they are striving for a complete union with "God" or the "divine" and that the identity, individuality and everything about the occultist is absorbed into the greater "God". The Left-Hand Path believes that they are to be self-deified and as such maintain their own identity and identification. To them, all humans are their own self-identified gods that are separate from one another.[39]

The problem seems to be clear here. If the semi-divine Nephilim could essentially become demons and/or gods, then the claims of the occult are given genuine legitimacy. This of course cannot be. While this cannot be the

---

37. Albert H. Newman, "Introductory Essay on the Manichæan Heresy," in *The Writings Against the Manichaeans and Against the Donatists Part I – The Manichaeans*, ed. Philip Schaff (Ingersoll, Ontario: Devoted Publishing, 2019), 21-25.

38. David Conway, *Magic: An Occult Primer* (Newport, Rhode Island: The Witches Almanac LTD, 2016), 44-46.

39. Kennet Granholm, *Embracing the Dark: The Magic Order of the Dragon Rouge – Its Practice in Dark Magic and Meaning Making* (Sarrijärvi, Suomi: Åbo Akademi University Press, 2005), 27-28.

only arguing point against the demonization of the Nephilim souls, the idea of self-deification has populated Western society to a level unseen in many years. If theologians hold to a position that something mortal, that has divinity in them can essentially become gods, people will start believing even more that the claims of the Bible are false.

Essentially, the lie of the serpent in Eden comes right back around to the fullest realization of that lie, "you will be like God" (Genesis 3:5 ESV)

Chapter III - The Testing of Job (Job 1-2:10, Job 42)

The testing of Job is primarily focused on the texts of Job 1-2:10. The majority of Job shows the response to suffering that Job has to respond to, but the beginning of the book deals with the origin of that suffering. While there are many different views on the interpretation of this section of Job, there needs to be a determination of these texts for the sake of the thesis. One point of discussion is in the person of Satan.[1] Since the Satan referred to here is indeed the enemy of God, the archenemy of God's people, it is safe to assume that Satan is at God's mercy when dealing with particular people under God's rule. Satan makes some accusations about the legitimacy of Job's faith. These accusations are based on the fact that Job is only righteous and loyal to God because of the enormous blessing that God (Yahweh) has given to him. Satan wants to challenge God to lift the veil of protection on Job so that Job's faith can really be put to the test. Satan, however, needs God's permission to do so.

To make the evidence clear that will point to the validity of the thesis, an exegesis will have to be done of Job 1-2:10 to formulate the argument. There is a lot to observe within the text, but the most important points will be highlighted. What will also be shown is an exegesis at the end of Job that will show the blessing poured out on Job for this righteousness. Where Satan intended to test Job to prove God wrong, God will show that Job's faith, and the testing that was inflicted on him will prove to be a testing that will ultimately benefit him. This whole process shows that God allowing Satan to test Job was shown as an act of sanctification and blessing.

First what must be observed is that Job was not perfect. Though the text upon a light reading may seem to make that case. Reading it carefully there are no indications that Job lived a perfect or sinless life. If Job had lived a sinless life, then the repentance at the end of the book would have been pointless. Since Job did in fact repent, it is reasonable to think that Job was

---

1. Many different arguments are made as to whether the Satan character in Job 1&2 is the same archfiend of the traditional belief of the "captain of Hell." The arguments are numerous and cannot be adequately argued for or against in the context of this paper. Many try to argue that the presence of the article "the" in the original Hebrew indicates that the "Satan" referred to here is a position within the heavenly court. Traditionally, this has never been the understanding. Different authors make the point one of which is David Clines whose work will be referenced in the main argument. As well, the most popular scholar holding to this view is Michael Heiser. In Heiser's famous book *The Unseen Realm* (p. 57) he makes the argument about the divine council and "the Satan" being part of that divine council. While these arguments are numerous, there is simply not the space in a paper of this size to appropriately deal with them. To state the point simply, I am taking the view that the Satan referred to in Job 1&2 truly is the demonic archfiend Satan that is the archenemy of the people of God. While there are numerous arguments for and against this view, it will simply have to do that this is the position taken.

in fact not a perfect man like the text upon a surface reading may imply.² In the end with the above said, the case here is that Job is not immediately assumed to be perfect. If Job were truly perfect, then Satan would have no grounds for tempting Job. Even though Job was not perfect in the common sense of the word, there is still a sense in which Job is suffering in a way he does not deserve. The only reason that Job is suffering in this way is because God has allowed it³ for his ultimate glory and the sanctification of Job. Job did not in any way deserve the disasters that Satan was delivering on him. What is interesting about this observation is that disaster will often fall on a Christian leaving them thinking "what have I done to deserve this?" This text indicates that in a sinful world, bad things can happen even to those who have not actually sinned. While Job was still in a sinful state where he had not done anything existentially wrong, he was also in a position that testing was warranted. God will test us with disaster, including from demonic hosts, to prove our faith and to sanctify us, much in the way God did Job.

How the event opens up is that the sons of God come and present themselves to God. In this event

> *The sons of God* (Heb. bənê hā'ĕlōhîm) are the celestial beings or angels whom God created as his servants. On this day they came and presented themselves (Heb. hityaṣṣēb) as courtiers to give an accounting of their activities to God.⁴ (italics original)

There are different beliefs about the sons of God,⁵ but in this occasion, it is clear they are angels of God. Among the presentation of the sons of God was the person of Satan. "The phrase among them has been interpreted as showing that the Satan was a regular member of the court ... This is going too far. In many places the preposition among is used to refer to an intruder."⁶ While arguments have been made for the fact that Satan may have been a regular member of what is referred to as "the divine council," Satan's words with God seems at odds with this conclusion.

The indication of the intentions of Satan in the challenge towards Job are of interest. Satan is in no way an all-power or infinite being. Many have assumed that Satan has restricted access to the earth and to even the lives of unbelievers and this is not the case. What is shocking with Job is that there were no foreseeable, from a reader's perspective, limits to the punishment Satan could inflict on Job excluding harming Job physically in any way. This amount of access to Job that Satan is granted could be seen as a threat to God,

---

2. Robert L. Alden, *Job*, vol. 11, *The New American Commentary* (Nashville, Tennessee: Broadman & Holman Publishers, 1993), 47-48.

3. David J. A. Clines, *Job 1–20*, vol. 17, *Word Biblical Commentary* (Dallas, Texas: Word, Incorporated, 1989), 8.

4. John E. Hartley, *The Book of Job, The New International Commentary on the Old Testament* (Grand Rapids, Michigan: Wm. B. Eerdmans Publishing Co., 1988), 71.

5. In Genesis 6, the sons of God have three basic explanations: 1) fallen angels, 2) kings and rulers, or 3) the godly line of Seth.

6. Francis I. Andersen, *Job: An Introduction and Commentary*, vol. 14, *Tyndale Old Testament Commentaries* (Downers Grove, Illinois: InterVarsity Press, 1976), 87.

but God is always in control and knew exactly how far Satan could and would go. In the end, Satan is shown and appears to be weak and pathetic against the power of God.[7] There has been a common belief in the history of the church that Satan has free reign (meaning authority) of the world. The text observed makes it clear this is not the case. While Satan may be able to do certain things free from God's will, ultimately, he is subjected to God's rule and the rule of the church. Even within the context of non-believers it is possible that since they possess the image of God that Satan may not have complete free reign on all of unsaved humanity. Since Satan does not have free reign over all the earth a reader has to realize that "This accuser is about to challenge Job's authenticity as a God-fearer, and at this point it is not yet clear whether he is making an accurate accusation."[8] Longman in this quote assumes, like Heiser, that Satan in this text is an office rather than the enemy of God, but if what Longman is suggesting is true, it speaks to a being trying to challenge one of God's chosen. Not an attribute that an unfallen angel would seek to do.

In addressing why Satan was present with the sons of God, the dialect suddenly changes so that Job becomes the target of God's inquiry. God may be showing some joy in the faithfulness of Job, but Satan wants to question God's premise. Satan does this by directly asking God "Then Satan answered the LORD and said, 'Does Job fear God for no reason?'" (Job 1:9 ESV) When we consider what Satan is saying to God, that God is essentially purchasing Job's worship. Without these promises of gifts of blessing, God would not deserve to be worshipped by Job, or by anyone.[9] Satan is accusing Job of having false faith. This false faith accusation is based on the fact that Job believes because he has his hearts desire. It is ironic how in prosperity and Word-Faith churches this same accusation is the basis of their theology. In those two cases, they believe, only so that they can reap the awards of that faith. In their context, the Word-Faith churches have failed the test of Job.

The next thing to observe is the intention of Satan's accusation. While it often is interpreted as indicated above, there is another way of looking at Satan's challenge. It could be said that "[s]uspicious of Job's reasons for fearing God, the Satan challenged Yahweh to test Job's fidelity. Using imperatives as though he were ordering Yahweh, he sought to force Yahweh to test Job."[10] Satan was trying to once again force himself as superior to the God of heaven. While God does allow Satan to test Job, it is not because of Satan's command, it is because God in the end knows what will happen and the intention behind God allowing it is not yet made clear. While Satan may be trying to force God to test Job "[h]e can do only what God permits him to do."[11]

---

7. Alden, *Job*, 53-54.
8. Tremper Longman III, *Baker Commentary on the Old Testament: Job* (Grand Rapids, Michigan: Baker Academic, 2012), 82.
9. Alden, *Job*, 55.
10. Hartley, *Job*, 73.
11. Anderson, *Job*, 87.

In order to show Satan that he is wrong, God does allow the testing to go forward. "The Lord accepts the challenge. The Satan is given permission to do what he likes with all Job's property. But he must not touch Job's person. The Satan goes out, eager to get on with the mischief."[12] In the end, Satan's mischief fails and although Job loses his children and all of his source of wealth, Job refuses to curse God. Instead, Job faithfully declares that "Naked I came from my mother's womb, and naked shall I return. The LORD gave, and the LORD has taken away; blessed be the name of the LORD" (Job 1:21 ESV).

When the second chapter of Job begins, we have God essentially taunting Satan,

> God had said Job would not abandon his relationship with him even if his "rewards" were taken away, and sure enough, Job persisted. Note that God acknowledges that he was moved to injure Job by the accuser's persuasive speech. He does not say that he allows the accuser to injure him (though he did use the accuser as his agent), but takes responsibility himself.[13]

What is interesting is how God takes responsible for hurting Job. The text in Job 1 seems to say that it was Satan that inflicted the devastation, yet now we have God taking responsibility. God explains why he, may or may not have, directly done this to Job: "The Lord did have a good reason for hurting Job, namely to disprove the Satan's slander. ... The Satan's experiment was all for nothing."[14] God had proved his point, Satan lost and the wager in the end did nothing to prove Satan's accusation as true. The accusation only proved that Job was righteous.

Since Satan lost the bet, why does he reappear before God? Since God already knows what happened with Job and that Job did not rebuke God in any way, it may just be a way for the writer of Job to move the story along faster than taking the time to reiterate everything that just happened. A big moment does happen though in that it is God that says that Job held fast to his righteousness (Job 2:3).[15] It is significant that God is the one that declared Job righteous. If Satan had done it, it would not have had the same effect. Since God, the Almighty One, declared this righteousness, it makes it certain. There can be no question about it. This also indicates that "He would not concede any of his authority to the Satan."[16] If Satan was the one that declared Job righteous, then it would indicate the Satan has an authority that God had never given him.

Since Satan's original wager has been lost, Satan comes before God to rechallenge the righteousness of Job. Satan has no choice but to concede that Job is righteous within the constraints that God had put on Satan. "Skin for

---

12. Anderson, *Job*, 90.
13. Longman, *Job*, 87.
14. Anderson, *Job*, 95.
15. Clines, *Job*, 41-42.
16. Hartley, *Job*, 80.

skin! All that a man has he will give for his life. But stretch out your hand and touch his bone and his flesh, and he will curse you to your face" (Job 2:4-5 ESV). The implication here is evident. Satan is accusing God of protecting Job and because of that protection Job is not fearful for his life. Make Job fearful for his life, then Job will curse God. Even though God does not allow Satan to kill Job, there is still a point at which

> Although Yahweh rejected the Satan's reasoning, he released Job into the Satan's power for further testing. But again he set a boundary to the affliction by prohibiting the Satan from taking Job's life. This concession reveals the full extent of God's confidence in Job, namely, that Job's basic commitment is to God alone.[17]

Even though Satan could not take Job's life, it does not mean that Job would not fear for his life considering the afflictions in his flesh. In the end Satan wanted Job to suffer every physical pain that he could inflict on him. Satan basically wanted God to allow him to show Job no mercy of any kind.[18] While Satan knew he could not take Job's life, Satan may have been hoping that Job would take his wife's curse in verse 9 to "curse God and die." In which case, Satan would win, and God would lose the second test.

Just as in chapter one with the first test, once again God gives Satan permission to inflict Job with another test. "Once more it is the Satan who is the agent. He is given authority (lit. hand) to do what he pleases, short of killing Job."[19] It is important to note that Satan could only act once God allowed him to. Without that permission given in verse 6, Satan would be powerless to afflict someone under God's authority. Just as the quote from Hartley in footnote 17 shows, God was confident in Job. This was an opportunity not only to prove Satan wrong, but to test Job in his righteousness, and in the end sanctify him and show who really is in control of the situation. In doing this it is interesting to think about how Job would have handled the situation. Job most likely did not see this as a sanctifying event.

> The shadow of death will fall over him so heavily that he will think that he is afflicted by a terminal illness with no hope of recovery. In this way God allows Job's faith to be tested to its innermost core.[20]

Christians will often not show the similar kind of faith. In times of trouble, those who claim to have faith in God will take a time of testing, a time to refine sanctification, and wonder why God would do something so terrible to them. The enemy is as much under the sovereign God as the church is. If God wants to use the demons to refine his church, like he did with Job, it is his sovereign right to do so.

---

17. Hartley, *Job*, 81.
18. Alden, *Job*, 64-65.
19. Anderson, *Job*, 96.
20. Hartley, *Job*, 81.

The extent to how much Job was suffering is evident in verses 7 and 8. The Satan at this point drops out of the picture and it turns to Job, his wife for a few verses and then his unfaithful friends. What is interesting is what Job's wife says to him. She demands that Job "curse God and die" (Job 2:9b ESV). This book to this point has been showing how Satan was being used to sanctify the person of Job. Here, whether it was Satan's influence, or just an instance of fallen humanity, Job's wife criticizes Job and tells him to do what Satan is trying to get Job to do in the first place. Understandably, she has lost everything because of the testing of Job. It does not take lengthy studies to understand why she would say something like this to her husband.

> Job's wife becomes an unknowing agent of the accuser when she urges her husband to end his piety (maintaining his innocence) and curse God. Notice that she does not deny his innocence. Rather, she chastises him for persisting in it.[21]

The text does not say directly that Job's wife was influenced by Satan, but there is a sense in which she is asking Job to admit his guilt and be done with it. "Her question could be a taunt. 'Do you still insist on maintaining your integrity? What good has it done you?' If so, she has already lost faith, and wants Job to join her."[22]

Moving to Job 42, a reader can start to see how Job comes to repent of the wrongs he ended up committing in his mournful state, and in the end, God brings elevated blessings and sanctification to Job. It is dangerous to assume that the sanctification that God brought Job was realized in the physical blessings and greater prosperity given to Job. While a connection in Old Testament terms can be made to the two, the two blessings are distinctively different. Before this book moves forward into Job 42, a statement of conviction must be made that the sanctification process given to Job in this chapter, is existentially different then the material blessings and greater prosperity given to Job as a reward for righteousness.

In the first part of his repentant statement in verses 1-6 it can be observed that Job knew how amazing this revelation of the all-powerful and all-loving God really was. Even in the midst of the greatest turmoil of Job's life Job acknowledges that God is the one in control and further readings of the end of Job recognize that we as humans have no right to question God in what he decides is for our good. Since God has his plans set, those same plans will be realized. There is nothing we can do about it. Any attempt to thwart the plans of God would essentially to be committing the very sin that Satan was tormenting Job to do.[23] Job is recognizing here that in the end, God is in control. While the idea that "God can do all things" is more of a statement of his power, within the statement is a moral claim as well that God as God is able to test us in any way that he chooses. In the end God cannot be thwarted.

---

21. Longman, *Job*, 89.
22. Anderson, *Job*, 98.
23. Alden, *Job*, 408.

Justice in the end is part of who God is and what he does to and for his creation. God gets to decide in all ways what that justice looks like. God is not subjected to particular outcomes or formulae to determine what punishment serves the crime. It is in every way up to the Almighty One of the created order what to do in any given situation. Job comes to realize this. Since Job was a sinful man, and not a perfect man, this understanding of God may have been lacking in Job's heart. Now Job knows in every sense that God, Yahweh, is the one that decides the outcome of any situation.[24] It is interesting here that Clines (see footnote 24) is showing a wisdom in Job that the church has often forgotten. God is allowed to do as he wishes. God is not bound by present-day, or ancient-day, human morality. If God in his holiness decides to test his people, God's justice is what allows that to happen. The church must be glad for that kind of testing, as it allows us to be refined and sanctified. If God were not the one in control of that show of justice, the testing could go horribly wrong at any moment. With God in control, there is a purpose and hope within the time of difficulty. This is a hope Christians today have decided to forget.

Since the unrighteousness of Job's friends is not argued in this book, there will not be a large discourse on it. Instead, what will be mentioned is that God uses the friends rebuke of Job to justify what Job was saying and believing.

> God does not deal with them according to their folly. Job is clearly pronounced to have had the better of the debate [...]. We have rested a great deal of our interpretation on this result. Job's vindication over against them is made public.[25]

God affirms that Job was in the right by not giving into the friends' pressure to rebuke God. This show of righteousness is what God was hoping for. It could be argued that Job's friends were also agents of Satan, much like Job's wife could have been, but Job proves that the faith that God knew Job had is true and vindicated.

Moving to the actual blessings given to Job starting in verse 10:

> The blessing proves that Yahweh is a life-giving God, not a capricious deity who takes pleasure in the suffering of those who fear him. In his sovereign design he may permit a faithful servant to suffer ill-fortune for a season, but in due time he will bring total healing. Moreover, the doubling symbolizes Yahweh's full acceptance of Job.[26]

As was mentioned before moving into chapter 42, the blessings given to Job was not a "reward" for Job's faithfulness. Hartley in the above quote shows

---

24. David J. A. Clines, *Job 38–42*, vol. 18B, *Word Biblical Commentary* (Nashville, Tennessee: Thomas Nelson, 2011), 1215.
25. Anderson, *Job*, 316.
26. Hartley, *Job*, 540.

that the material blessing was a symbol of God's acceptance of Job. To read that if Christians suffer for a season and expect to be materially blessed is a misreading of God's acceptance of Job. The original Hebrew readers would most likely not have accepted that interpretation. It was a sign that before the divine council, before Satan, and before the world, that Job was accepted and declared righteous before God. Job had been tested and proved to have been sanctified in his suffering.

Observing all the texts relevant to the thesis in Job is extensive and cannot be done fully in the context of this book. Space is always limiting and makes it difficult. The point has been shown in a brief way, that Satan was limited from just going after Job at his own whim. Job recognized in chapter 42 that God is ultimately in control and able to do anything he desires for his own sense of justice. It can be argued that God desired for Satan to test Job. God was the one that mentioned to the great adversary of whether Satan had "considered" Job. It is not wrong to read this as a statement of pride God is showing towards Job's faithfulness, but since God is sovereign and is foreknowing in all things, God knew full well that Satan was going to challenge the standing of Job before God. Once Satan did that, God knew that Job was not going to crumble under the loss of family, possessions, riches and even his health. Job may not have been kept truly innocent in the entirety of the text of Job, but Job does repent at the end, proving his sanctification and the ultimate loss of Satan in the testing against Job.

Job came out sanctified in the end. This does not belittle the idea that God used Satan to do this end game of sanctification. The testing would only do one of two things: 1) prove that Job was as righteous as God knew he was, or 2) prove that Job was not righteous and that he was to be condemned. Satan could not have foreseen how this would turn out. In the end, Satan was unwillingly used to do exactly what God had wanted in testing Job. The text itself shows that Satan could not have done these tests without the sovereign God's permission. Since God knew what the outcome would be, it is evidence that Satan willingly undertook the test to prove God wrong, but in the end was doing a process of sanctification that, if Satan had known, would have been an unwilling event. It cannot be denied that Satan does have certain amount of prideful autonomy. The fact that he tried to overthrow God, to claim God's throne as his own, is evidence of this. In the end, since Satan does not possess complete autonomy, he is subject to God's rule.

Chapter IV - Peter, and the Apostles, being "sifted like wheat" (Luke 22:31-38)

At this point, the exegesis shifts to the New Testament text of Luke 22:31-38. In this text a bold statement is made by Christ. This statement is essentially that Satan has asked to sift, not just Peter but all the apostles, like wheat (v. 31). The purpose of this is to test each apostle to determine their ability to persevere in the faith. What is historically noticeable is that all but one of the apostles are eventually martyred. In the proof text of Job, Job's life was on purposely spared, but in these texts, Satan has asked to sift them. This sifting is hinted to be quite severe. In the end, the sifting will claim all but one of the apostles' lives. Yet, within that martyrdom, the apostles will prove to be sanctified, even in the face of failure. The proof text mentions all apostles to begin with, but then singles out Peter at the end of it. Jesus specifically mentions that he has prayed for Peter that Peters' faith will not fail. There are implications within that statement. Implications not that Peter will become apostate, but that his faith will not fail him in his pursuit of living for Christ and pursuing sanctification. As Jesus will say at the last verse, Peter will fail in the next few verses, which is part of Peters' eventual sanctification.

The opening verse 31 seems to indicate that Jesus is talking directly to Peter, and that the sifting Satan is asking for is directed at Peter alone. This is simply a misinterpretation of the Greek. Granted, English words do not have different singular and plural words for "you", and this is the reason this opening statement is often misread.

> In Satan's prayer to have you, you is plural and includes all the disciples. The Greek appears to mean 'Satan has obtained you by asking': there is the thought that the petition has been granted. In passing we notice that Satan has no rights here; he may ask, but it is God who is supreme. It follows that the trials and testings that come to God's people are only those that he allows. The metaphor of sifting like wheat is unparalleled, but it is obvious that it signifies great trials.[1]

With the Greek properly indicating that Satan has asked to sift all the apostles, the eventual death of them seems to have a common source. While this can be easily argued just on the martyrdom of the apostles itself, the statement by Jesus makes it evident that the apostles needed to know what was going to happen beforehand. In giving this warning, Jesus wanted them to keep the faith and be sanctified in their ministries. What is a more critical point, is that

---

1. Leon Morris, *Luke: An Introduction and Commentary*, vol. 3, Tyndale New Testament Commentaries (Downers Grove, Illinois: InterVarsity Press, 1988), 327.

Satan had to ask God the Father for this testing and sifting to take place. Satan could not accomplish these tasks without the Father saying it was permitted.

There is hope in what Jesus clears up in verse 32. Jesus has intervened, not just for Peter, but all the apostles. While Peter is the direct object of the prayer, Jesus wants Peter to know that Jesus has prayed that the Father will not allow Peters' faith to fail. Jesus knows very well that Satan will throw everything the archfiend can at the apostle. Jesus wants Peter to know that for him specifically, and in the end all the apostles, to remain strong in the faith that Peter has.[2] It is also interesting to note that according to Nolland, Jesus expected that Peter should lead the example of faith to the rest of the apostles in the sifting to come. Having Peter perform this role, with the failings he will have shown to committed, is an interesting affirmation of trust in Peter by Christ. Also, the prayer indicates that Jesus did not want Peters' faith to waver either in the attacks to be expected by the devil. It is clear that Jesus' statement is making the apostles all aware that Satan is going to try and unsettle them. Jesus does not want that to happen.[3] Thankfully, in Jesus also being fully God, Jesus knew the apostles in the end would remain faithful.

Satan is most likely at this time expecting that at least some of the apostles will fail the test of faith. The pronouncement by Jesus about Peter denying Jesus three times would fuel that argument. But again, Satan does not seem to be aware of the purposes of God. Just like with Job, God had a purpose in proving Job's righteousness. So here again, God is using this moment of Satan trying to test the apostles to ultimately prove their faith.

> Not even this is sufficient ultimately to frustrate God's redemptive purpose. Peter and the others will temporarily succumb, but they will recover; what is more, far from thwarting the divine will, the events now unfolding are actually caught up in God's intention.[4]

This is clear also in that like with Job, Jesus here is praying for intercession with Peter, and the apostles. Satan may expect that he will succeed in drawing the apostles to apostasy but "it is more probable that Luke understood it rightly as being that Satan would not be able totally to destroy Peter's faith; the process of sifting would not lead to its intended end."[5] Jesus was well aware that Peter would not commit apostasy and that the rejection of Jesus by Peter at the denial incident is not that Peter loses his faith completely. Jesus knows that in the near future the apostle will swear to Jesus that he will not fall away. As will be shown in the next pericope, Peter does deny Jesus. At this moment however, Peter does not know that and wants to assure his

---

2. John Nolland, *Luke 18:35–24:53, vol. 35C, Word Biblical Commentary* (Dallas, Texas: Word, Incorporated, 1993), 1072.

3. Robert H. Stein, *Luke, vol. 24, The New American Commentary* (Nashville, Tennessee: Broadman & Holman Publishers, 1992), 552.

4. Joel B. Green, *The Gospel of Luke, The New International Commentary on the New Testament* (Grand Rapids, Michigan: Wm. B. Eerdmans Publishing Co., 1997), 771.

5. I. Howard Marshall, *The Gospel of Luke: A Commentary on the Greek Text, New International Greek Testament Commentary* (Exeter: Paternoster Press, 1978), 821.

Lord that it will not happen.⁶ Peter tries to reaffirm his faith, in the short-term Satan's sifting will prove effective, however, Jesus knows that Peter will not completely reject the faith. In the end, Peter will die for the faith that he pretended not to believe in by denying Christ.

Is the denial of Christ the only time that Peter fails? It does not seem to be. In Galatians 2:11-14 Paul rebukes Peter for refusing to eat with Gentiles in the presence of Jews. If Jews were not around then there is "This picture of Cephas enjoying unreserved table-fellowship (which included participation in the memorial breaking of bread) with the Gentile members of the Antiochene church."⁷ Paul rebukes Peter and calls him to repent because Peter was determining his own righteousness by the standards of the Torah law. Since this law is no longer that measure, with the filling-up of Christ of that law, the most important thing to remember was Peters' relationship with Jesus and not adherence to the Mosaic Law.⁸

When Paul rebukes Peter it can be seen that Peter knew what he had done. This error by Peter was not something done in vain or ignorance. While Peter had also in no way denied that salvation also extended to the Gentile believers, Peter was still showing a mask of Torah self-righteousness. Since Peter knew better than to think or act this way, he knew his own error. Because Peter had shown hypocritical actions with his teaching and convictions, Paul stepped up to call him to repent.⁹ Since Peter had made a public sin, Paul was most likely to rebuke Peter "[because] the offence was public, [so] the rebuke had also to be public."¹⁰ Jesus had told his followers to rebuke people privately before publicly. The quote by Bruce makes it clear why Paul contradicted this requirement.

In the end the text of Galatians does not tell us that Peter did in fact repent. It is most likely that Peter did. If Peter was to die the martyr's death that he did, then it can be considered a confirmed account that Peter did repent to Paul and be reconciled to his state of sanctification. Satan's sifting was continuing even in this time of the gospel's spread. Peter still was not perfect and in need of the sanctifying process the sifting would produce.

The testimony of the early church speaks of the ministry of Peter after the testimony of the Bible. "Peter was crucified under Nero and makes passing reference to the widely attested claim that the apostle repeatedly opposed Simon Magus in Rome after Simon had abandoned his pretense of Christian faith."¹¹ Peter opposed false teaching in the area of Rome and taught correct doctrine instead of the falsehood brought on by heretics such as Simon Magus.¹² To support the ministry of Peter in Rome, early writers said, "the Gos-

---

6. Nolland, *Luke*, 1074.

7. F. F. Bruce, *The Epistle to the Galatians: A Commentary on the Greek Text*, New International Greek Testament Commentary (Grand Rapids, Michigan: W.B. Eerdmans Pub. Co., 1982), 129.

8. Timothy George, *Galatians*, vol. 30, The New American Commentary (Nashville, Tennessee: Broadman & Holman Publishers, 1994), 174.

9. George, *Galatians*, 177.

10. Bruce, *Galatians*, 132.

11. Markus Bockmuehl, *Simon Peter in Scripture and Memory: The New Testament Apostle in the Early Church* (Grand Rapids, Michigan: Baker Academic, 2012), 103.

pel of Matthew was written while Peter and Paul were evangelizing and strengthening the church in Rome,"[13] This claim may or not be true, but once again, it speaks to the influence of Peter on the early church. This influence is evident that the sifting inflicted by Satan, was in the end sanctifying Peter.

An interesting fact about Peter is that "Peter asked to be crucified with his head downwards, because he did not feel worthy of dying in the same posture as his Lord and Master."[14] This is a clear testimony to Peters' faithfulness and the eventual sanctification that he underwent until the day of his death. The influence of Peter on the church cannot be denied. Although the Roman Catholic Church claims that Peter was their first pope, the evidence does seem to be lacking. Regardless of that claim, the influence of Peter on the Roman church can still be seen and felt in the world today. Peter's testimony in Rome changed a lot of how Christians were coping with the persecutions of Rome.

> [W]ithin a generation or two of Peter's death in Rome, certain local Christian memories of him had gained sufficient currency that an early second-century pagan resident of the city could come across them and mistake them for descriptions of Christianity's founder.[15]

The influence of Peter in Rome was so great that he was almost regarded with Christ himself. Although that is ridiculous, it attests to the faithfulness and sanctification of Peter before and in the testimonies of him after his death.

The text of Luke 22:31-34 shows that all apostles were given to Satan to sift, but Peter was the target of the narrative. Peter soon after that proclamation of Satan by Christ denied Christ three times. Years later, he committed wrong in separating himself from Gentiles when around Jews. In the end however, despite Peters' failures as an apostle, and as a sinful man, he became one of the biggest influencers of the church in the first century. So much so, that even centuries after Peter was crucified upside down, people thought Peter had founded Christianity. Peter did not, but it speaks to Peters' level of sanctification as result of Satan's sifting.

---

12. Some early church fathers believed that Simon Magus was the founder of a sect of Gnosticism. While these claims may be true, it is not confirmed. If they are true, it could be believed that Peter was confronting Simon Magus and defending the faith against Gnostic thought. See Irenæus, *Against Heresies* (Ingersoll, Ontario: Devoted Publishing, 2020).

13. Bockmuehl, *Peter,* 103.

14. Viktor Rydberg, *Roman Legends about the Apostles Paul and Peter,* trans. Ottilia Von Düben (London, England: Elliot Stock, 1898), 89.

15. Bockmuehl, *Peter,* 108.

Excursus

The two former Bible passages exegeted were done so due to the direct evidence they offer to the thesis of this book. A reader of this book may wonder why the argument is going backwards from the New Testament back to passages in the Old Testament. As a matter of making the argument, the first two passages above are shown to be direct evidence of what the thesis is trying to argue. Bringing those to light will help to shed light on what is going on in other Old Testament passages where God seems to be giving permission to test for other reasons than sanctification, or to deny allowing Satan to test a member of the Jewish community. It is important to observe what these passages are saying in the greater context of the thesis, but they are showing something different, but still related in a slightly altered manner. The direct evidence was shown first, then the exceptions are to be discussed next. The idea to present the arguments in the order they are presented in the English Bible was considered, but this method was decided on instead.

Chapter V - God Allows a Spirit to Test to Condemn (1 Kings 22:13-28)

This text in 1 Kings is always one that seems to cause problems in demonology studies in the Old Testament. Some commentators have said that the spirit sent to put lies in the mouths of the false prophets was most definitely a demon. Others have made the argument that the spirit must have been an angel of God because a demon would not have been able to enter God's presence. Both arguments seem to have some relevance, but the stance taken here will be that the spirit was in fact a demon. In doing this, a reader can see that God is allowing a demon to test the king of Israel, Ahab, and the king of Judah, Jehoshaphat. What this testing was intended to bring out was God's condemnation, not sanctification. This is a drastic, but related, difference.

When the false prophets have said their false guarantees about the success of the campaign that Ahab and Jehoshaphat are planning, Micaiah then speaks. When he does: Micaiah is compelled to agree with other false prophets. Micaiah does reply in a way that says he can only say what God has told him to. So, when Micaiah speaks agreement with the other false prophets, Ahab knows not only Micaiah, but God is mocking him.[1] Ahab quickly picks on the prophet agreeing with the other false prophets. King Ahab makes that statement quite clearly that "How many times shall I make you swear that you speak to me nothing but the truth in the name of the LORD?" (1 Kings 22:16 ESV) Ahab was most likely feeling insulted by Micaiah making this mocking agreement. At the same time as this mocking agreement "[w]hen Micaiah merely repeated the false prophecy it could have been out of irony or to test Ahab's sincerity."[2] Regardless of how Micaiah intended this mocking agreement, it is clear that Micaiah knew that God was going to test especially Ahab in this moment. Ahab was clearly frustrated by this and insisted that Micaiah tell him what the Lord was really saying.

After another statement to test and lead Ahab astray, Ahab once more demands that Micaiah tell him the truth. In verse 19 Micaiah responds with a second vision form the Lord. Micaiah then explains a vision that he received from Yahweh. Micaiah describes that he has seen Yahweh on his throne with a whole host of other celestial beings. God is asking for spirits to fill the prophets' mouths with lies. None of the other heavenly beings will do so, so another spirit volunteers and is sent to do as Yahweh has commanded him.[3]

---

1. Paul R. House, *1, 2 Kings*, vol. 8, *The New American Commentary* (Nashville, Tennessee: Broadman & Holman Publishers, 1995), 236.

2. Donald J. Wiseman, *1 and 2 Kings: An Introduction and Commentary*, vol. 9, *Tyndale Old Testament Commentaries* (Downers Grove, Illinois: InterVarsity Press, 1993), 199.

3. Simon J. DeVries, *1 Kings*, 2nd ed., vol. 12, *Word Biblical Commentary* (Dallas, Texas: Word, Inc, 2003), 268.

This demonic being[4] is sent out to do as God has asked. When God asks the spirit what is planned, the spirt responds "I will go out, and will be a lying spirit in the mouth of all his prophets" (1 Kings 22:22 ESV). God seems pleased with that and sends the spirit out.

This shows very directly that God did not intend this testing to sanctify either Ahab or Jehoshaphat. In fact, it indicates that God has already condemned Ahab since this demon/spirit is being sent to essentially kill Ahab. These deceived false prophets will convince Ahab to put himself in a position that will claim his life.[5] This may seem extreme, but as was explained in the passage about Job 42, God's morality is not human morality. God as the ultimate and holy judge, is able to condemn or lift up whomever he chooses. Since Ahab had a history of rebellion against God, God had decreed judgment on him. When it comes to the evil Ahab had done during his reign of the northern kingdom of Israel, God is showing that he alone is the true king of Israel. God alone is truly sovereign. As such, nothing will go unnoticed by God and likewise, no one is able to do anything outside of God's divine sanction or justice. Everyone will answer for what they have done.[6] Ahab had operated outside of God's law for his entire life. Ahab and his marriage to Jezebel is evidence of this rebellion. God had enough of who could be called the most evil king of the northern kingdom, and the time for judgment had come. God was offering Ahab one more test, to turn around and do as God commanded. Ahab once again would fail and be judged.

A false prophet by the name of Zedekiah (a different person than the biblical prophet), gets angered at what Micaiah is saying and then slaps him.

> [T]his is a long used and recognized legal and symbolic act in making a public challenge to speak the truth (as with Jesus Christ in John 18:22). The inquiry Which way did the Spirit of (NIV mg.) or from the LORD go? may question either Micaiah's prophetic source or imply that anyone can make up lies.[7]

And at the same time Micaiah then pronouncing judgment on Zedekiah saying that in the end Zedekiah will know who the one that Yahweh has sent is. As a result, Zedekiah will hide in fear and be forced to face the truth about God and his own condemnation.[8] It can be guaranteed that since Zedekiah was prophesying falsely in the name of the Lord, that this warning and pronouncement of judgement by Micaiah was not taken seriously. Zedekiah most likely walked off proudly, assuming that his false beliefs were justified and true.

---

4. This is a lot of disagreement whether this lying spirit was really a demon. With the outcome and the intention of the spirit itself, it does send a clear message that this spirit was a holy angel. The message seems to be that it was in fact a fallen angel, a demon.

5. DeVries, *1 Kings*, 268.

6. House, *1, 2 Kings*, 238.

7. Wiseman, *1 and 2 Kings*, 200.

8. House, *1, 2 Kings*, 238.

Ahab responds in anger towards Micaiah. Since pagan beliefs were often highly involved in magic and other forms of ancient occultism, it is believable that Ahab thought Micaiah would do some kind of action or ritual to make the judgment happen. The king then demands that Micaiah be put into house arrest. The city governor and Prince Joash are put in charge to make sure Micaiah does no such ritual during his arrest. Micaiah will be given what he needs to survive. Once Ahab returns in safety the final judgment on Micaiah will be carried out. Until that time, Ahab does not want Micaiah performing some magical ritual to make happen what the prophet of God had said.[9] Ahab does give a term of release. The English may seem to say that Ahab if he comes back alive, then Micaiah will be released. "'Until I return in peace' (MT) may well be with a victory pact concluded rather than just safely (NEB, NIV)."[10] Ahab would be wanting to rub not just the fact he survived, but the fact that Ahab was victorious in Micaiah's face. In doing so, Ahab thought he would prove to Micaiah, and to God, that the prophecy issued against him was false. Ahab would then mockingly believe that the vision of a "lying spirit" would be the lie. The false prophet Zedekiah would be justified, and Ahab would walk away the winner.

Micaiah, whether out of concern or by the command of God, warns Ahab one more time in verse 28. Micaiah guarantees Ahab that he has spoken the truth. Micaiah is even willing to go so far as stake his reputation and everything he stands for to be given as collateral. In that day, that was a big risk to take.[11] This last warning is clear. Micaiah almost mockingly responds by saying that "If you return in peace, the LORD has not spoken by me" (1 Kings 22:28 ESV). The reader will know just reading the narrative that Micaiah was speaking the truth. The Lord had spoken words of testing and judgment against Ahab. For the time that Micaiah was in "[i]t is appropriate for the prophet as the prisoner to make this challenge to look for the confirmation of his prophecy."[12] It is likely this was a common plea to genuineness. Micaiah on this occasion was deadly serious.

Ahab in the end fails the test. Ahab was likely subject to many such pleas that "if what I say does not happen, then I am wrong." Even in today's world, many false prophets will make such claims. When they do not happen, it is ironic how they then claim, "it happened in the spiritual realm," whatever that may mean. Ahab however will not be fooled by what he thinks is a two-faced side of God and an assumed false prophet (Micaiah) making empty threats. Ahab's own personal experience makes him think this way. The king of northern Israel will take full responsibility for his own actions.[13] With Ahab being so defiant, it is ironic that the writer of 1 Kings shows that the prophecy given Micaiah could not be overturned or proved wrong. Ahab arrogantly thought he would be able to prove the prophet of God to be a liar.[14] As can

---

9. DeVries, *1 Kings*, 268.
10. Wiseman, *1 and 2 Kings*, 200.
11. House, *1, 2 Kings*, 238.
12. Wiseman, *1 and 2 Kings*, 200.
13. House, *1, 2 Kings*, 238.
14. DeVries, *1 Kings*, 268–269.

be read further from verse 29 onward, Ahab does fall under God's judgment for failing the testing that God issued to him. In his pagan state of thinking, Ahab had believed that Yahweh fell under similar pagan guidelines and limitations. God does not. Ahab may have tried to avert the consequences of the failed test by putting Micaiah in prison, but God's power is sovereign and not limited by the ritual actions of a human being.

It is also of note that even though Ahab was completely apostate in every sense of the word, the demon still needed Yahweh's permission to test Ahab. This may seem weird to "specialists" within biblical demonology circles. What it shows is that anyone under the covenant community needs to have permission given to a demonic creature for that person to be afflicted or tested. Even though Ahab and the entire northern kingdom of Israel were apostate and fallen, Yahweh had not yet severed, or divorced, them from the covenant. Northern Israel was still a covenant community. As such, the demonic still needed Yahweh's permission to test the apostate king and nation.

Within this text of 1 Kings 22:13-28 there is a fascinating use of demons to test apostate peoples, maybe in an attempt to warn them, call them back to repentance, but ultimately to call them to judgment. God frequently uses demonic beings to test the church, to sanctify them and cause them to grow in holiness by often brutal testing. Here, however, God is using a demon to fill the mouths of false prophets with lies, or more lies than before, to call an evil king of northern Israel to judgment. This kind of morality by God often brings many Bible translators to try and make alternate explanations to explain God in human terms. The fact is, God is sovereign, and the testimony of how God has not just used demons, but Satan himself, to purify his people is a biblical standard. It should not be absurd for God to send demons to deceive people. This deception is an ultimate judgment of the Almighty God. This last test is a way that God is giving the apostate person a last chance to repent, but in the end the test condemns.

Chapter VI - God Forbids that Satan Accuse the High Priest (Zechariah 3)

In this scene, another paradigm that proves that God is the one with the authority to test and sanctify the believing body is made clear. Different metaphors are being used of different individuals, but the case is clear: God is the one who can decide whether Satan is allowed to accuse and test a believing person. Since the purpose of testing, shown in Job 1-2:10 and Luke 22:31-38, is to sanctify and prove the faith of the saints, some cases where Satan wants to test the people of God would prove nothing and only be destructive in the end. The case laid out in Zechariah 3 shows that for whatever reason, God is not allowing Satan to even accuse Joshua. Joshua in this context may represent the people of Judah, but the point is still made. The ability of Satan to perform an accusing role is limited. The church throughout history has believed Satan to be an autonomous accuser, able to levy any accusation against a child of God. Zechariah 3 shows this is not the case. In a case where God is the one to impose the sanctification, Satan has no right to test or accuse.

The four characters introduced to the reader in Zechariah 3 are God, the angel of the Lord, Satan and the high priest Joshua. Some commentators have said that Joshua does not imply a single individual person but rather the nation of Judah as a whole.

> The scene is the heavenly court room, where the angel of the Lord, called simply 'the Lord' in verse 2, represents God as judge, and Joshua, who, in his official capacity as the high priest, represents the Jews, stands as prisoner in the dock. His accuser is Satan, a transliteration of the Hebrew word meaning 'adversary'.[1]

A definite sense here is that Joshua, if he is representing the entire Jewish nation, is on trial before God, and Satan is the official accuser against him. The implication is that Joshua is dirty and filthy, probably for the sins that sent Judah into exile in the first place. Satan is trying to accuse the Jewish people as not being worthy of sanctification, and restoration as Gods' people.

Although the setting occurs in heaven, not a courtroom, the text has a judicial flavor. Joshua, the defendant, whose fouled vestments portray his own defilement, also epitomizes sinful Judah. If the high priest is so filthy, how much more the nation as a whole.[2] When dealing with this situation, the

---

1. Joyce G. Baldwin, *Haggai, Zechariah and Malachi: An Introduction and Commentary*, vol. 28, *Tyndale Old Testament Commentaries* (Downers Grove, Illinois: InterVarsity Press, 1972), 120.

2. George L. Klein, *Zechariah, vol. 21B, The New American Commentary* (Nashville,

angel of the Lord needs to prove that Judah is worthy of God's forgiveness and sanctification. What we must note, is that God refuses to give into Satan's accusation.

There must be a reason that God does not give in to Satan's accusation and rebukes Satan to turn him away from trying to bring guilt on Joshua, and Judah. "This suggests that some part of his accusation was false, although with no record of the accuser's words it is impossible to determine what was false in the witness."[3] While it may take some imaginative thinking to come to a conclusion about what Satan was saying about Joshua, the fact that Satan was even there serves as proof alone that Joshua was not qualified for service to the Lord. Something he had done, or some unclean state he was in, was enough to remove him from temple duty.[4] Since Yahweh refused to allow Satan to accuse Joshua, no matter what these damning accusations were, God was not going to condemn Joshua, or call him unworthy based off something that Satan may have said that was not accurate or true to Gods' promises to his chosen people.

Since Satan has been rebuked in verse 2, Yahweh who is someone that "on the other [side] stands a force who has chosen out of his sovereign mercy (see 1:16–17), and through this choice has announced a new era. It is such a theocentric focus which would be key to the success of the restoration project"[5] God had determined that Joshua and Judah were going to stand as righteous before him. This means that the accusation of Satan had no grounding in God's justice. In doing so, God has rebuked Satan in such a way that "The reference to a brand plucked from the fire recalls Amos 4:11; evidently this was a proverbial saying to indicate privileged deliverance from God's providential chastisements."[6] Whether or not Satan's accusation was somehow wrong, or not aligned to the promises of God to his people, God decided to not allow Satan's accusations to have merit and to deliver Joshua from the condemnation that he could have received for possibly not being worthy or "clean" enough to serve as high priest.

The proof of Joshua's unclean state is the focus of the next verse. In verse 3 it describes Joshua as "clothed with filthy garments" (Zechariah 3:3b ESV). This is important because under Mosaic Law "Such a state was inappropriate for an Israelite who desired to remain in the community, let alone the high priest, who was given charge of the holiest precincts and articles in Judah and would enter Yahweh's most holy presence."[7] The totality of what Satan was accusing Joshua of may have not been accurate, but Joshua was still standing in the divine trial in an unsuitable state to serve as the high priest. Similarly, Judah was not clean and could not serve as God's people. Joshua knew he

---

Tennessee: B & H Publishing Group, 2008), 133.

   3. Mark J. Boda, *The Book of Zechariah*, ed. R. K. Harrison and Robert L. Hubbard Jr., The New International Commentary on the Old Testament (Grand Rapids, Michigan: W. B. Eerdmans Publishing Company, 2016), 233.

    4. Klein, *Zechariah*, 133.

    5. Boda, *Zechariah*, 233-234.

    6. Baldwin, *Zechariah*, 121.

    7. Boda, *Zechariah*, 236.

was not clean and worthy to serve God as high priest. The filth of his clothing indicates just how bad and/or unclean he was. In the end, the doctrinal significance of Joshua's state is something we have to take seriously to understand what is happening here.[8] Joshua knew he was not worthy to serve God and his embarrassment is evident.

Since God has rebuked Satan and not allowed him to accuse God's high priest, God must act to make Joshua worthy and clean enough to be God's representative on earth. Since Joshua, as a representative of Judah, was carrying all the wrongs, moral and legal, upon his shoulders, it is a great sign of grace that Joshua now carries the grace and forgiveness of God. The people of Judah have paid the price of their pre-exilic crimes against God. This show of forgiveness is significant in many ways as it allows for any taint or perversion from living in a foreign land for so long to be ceremonially wiped away.[9] God did not need to have Joshua, or Judah, to prove themselves in another test. God did not need the people of the covenant to be tested any further to prove their innocence and righteousness. The people of Judah had carried out the punishment that God inflicted on them faithfully and had cried out to God as he wanted in order to once again sanctify them. What is exceedingly interesting is that God does not just clean and purify Joshua and the people of Judah, "But that was not all. [God] will clothe [Joshua] with rich apparel promised garments suitable for the heavenly court, which it would have been beyond Joshua's power to provide."[10] Joshua was not capable of being the priest that God required him to be. Satan knew this as well as Joshua and God, but God still rebuked Satan from accusing and testing Joshua and reached down out of his own glory, allowing God to make Joshua just not clean, but completely able to enter the presence of God as though nothing had happened.

Now that God has removed Joshua's guilt, sanctifying him once again for service in the presence of the Lord, God's next speech is made and

> this address announces a bilateral agreement which makes the promise dependent on fulfillment of demands. The gracious act of removal of guilt provides the conditions for a new start for Joshua (and Jerusalem and the people), but this will entail a response from the priest.[11]

God is making a covenant with Joshua that is conditional upon Joshua's fulfillment of it. So long as Joshua fulfills the promises of the Mosaic Covenant and the reassurance given here, then Joshua, or Judah, will rule the courts of God and have access to God's house (verse 7). While God was expecting the priesthood itself to fulfill the requirements of the law in the Torah, the priesthood was now being given authority over the civil aspects of

---

8. Klein, *Zechariah*, 137-138.
9. Klein, *Zechariah*, 140.
10. Baldwin, *Zechariah*, 122.
11. Boda, *Zechariah*, 244.

Judah as well. Since the king had been removed, an authority needed to oversee the people. This was supposed to remain in place until the rightful king came.[12] Since the Davidic king was not re-established after the exile, someone needed to fulfill the role of king. God gave the priests this responsibility until the rightful king would come. This made the readers and people of Judah wonder when will the Davidic king return.

God answers this question in Zechariah 3:8-10 in the coming Branch that will remove the iniquity of the land in a day. This we know was the person of Jesus. Joshua would not have understood that this was the person of someone named "Jesus," but he would have seen a prophetic promise in this statement.

> While Joshua may have been focused on the many responsibilities he was now commissioned to fulfill, he is forced immediately to think of the role of another figure. Both the previous commission (v. 7) and, initially, the present prophetic word are addressed to Joshua as leader of the renewed priestly caste.[13]

The end of Zechariah 3 promises the coming of the "Branch" (verse 8), the stone with seven eyes (verse 9), and the removal of the iniquity of the land (again verse 9) What Zechariah was thinking was that only one Davidic king would come that would fulfill the Messianic hopes of the Old Testament and the people of Judah.[14] The promised king given to David in 2 Samuel 7:1-29 was a hope Israel and Judah had hoped in for centuries. Again, God is promising that if the nation remains faithful, the Branch, the Messiah will come.

What has been seen in this exegesis is that Satan was denied the chance to accuse and test Joshua and the Jews because God was aware that something within Satan's desire was not based on complete truth or on the promises of God to the Jewish people. God promised them that he would restore Judah to the land. In rebuking Satan, God made it clear that he was the one that was going to cleanse Joshua and the Jewish people. By rebuking Satan, God also made it clear that it was his desire in this cleaning to bring the Messiah to the people. God did not want Satan to test the people because there was a purpose behind it. This promise of the Messiah was to be given, the only way for Judah to be clean and bring the Messiah was not to test them but to declare them clean. Satan's testing would not have been productive because, unless God intervened in the spiritual state of the Jews, the people would never have been sanctified enough to bring the Messiah to the throne of David. Satan was not in a place to challenge God's plan.

---

12. Klein, *Zechariah*, 142.
13. Boda, *Zechariah*, 252.
14. Klein, *Zechariah*, 145.

Chapter VII - The Testing of the Church in History

It has been shown that testing from God using the demonic is a standard laid out in the Bible. Job and Luke both include passages where Satan directly asks for permission to test someone in a stance of righteousness before God. Demonologists in the Christian tradition will often hear accusations that the time of demonic oppression is over. It ended after the closing of the canon. Is this true? It is a hard conclusion to come to. Many testimonies of demonic oppression and possession have been made by many people over the last two thousand years. If the people of God, and of the world are being tested in this way, then it can be argued that the church as a body of believes has been as well. The martyrdom of the early saints during the Roman Empire, the death of Reformers at the time of the Reformation as well as the growth and persecution of the church today will be observed and shown that these events, most likely demonic[1] in origin, are proving the church to continue in the process of sanctification.

The persecution of the early church in the first couple centuries AD is undisputed. The causes are numerous and when seen today are often mocked and seen as unbelievable. The reasons for execution of the Christian church was a reality to the early believers and even non-believers in Rome.

As brutal as this period was to early Christians, the gospel could not be stopped. The Christians were becoming such a problem in the pagan sphere of Rome that they felt that something had to be done about them. At the famous incident of the burning of Rome in 64 AD by the emperor Nero, it was not hard for him to blame the Christians since they were mostly in a state of disfavour anyway. "If the followers of Jesus had not conceived of themselves as a discrete group before the fire of Rome, Nero's dramatic response forced them to define themselves as Christians."[2] Even during the ministry of Paul at Philippi it is notable that "aggrieved pagans and aggrieved Jews found themselves united in the plea that Paul and his companions were preaching ideas which were incompatible with loyalty to the Roman Empire."[3] It is not difficult to conclude that the church was being killed and expelled from com-

---

1. As with other arguments about the Nephilim, the person of Satan and others above, this is a thesis all on its own that cannot be fully developed here. Is all evil demonic in origin? It is difficult to say that with surety. Since the church is such a representation of Christ on earth, it should not be a difficult conclusion to think that when the church is on the verge of moral or social collapse, something happens that sanctifies the church once again. These attacks can most certainly be presumed to be demonic in origin.

2. Candida R. Moss, *Ancient Christian Martyrdom: Diverse Practices, Theologies, and Traditions* (London, England: Yale University Press, 2012), 77.

3. W. H. C. Frend, *Martyrdom and Persecution in the Early Church: A Study of the Conflict from the Maccabees to Donatus* (Grand Rapids, Michigan: Baker Book House, 1981), 158.

munities for being a new religion, and also preaching a gospel that taught that Jesus was Lord and not Caesar. Such a preaching would put any governor on guard. To have someone teaching that someone else is Lord in their region could bring the wrath of Caesar in the Roman Legions. While persecution was fairly limited in certain areas to begin with, it did spread as the centuries led on.

Since Satan would have needed God's permission to test and persecute the church, it is evident that the church was being persecuted right to their deaths. Unlike Job, Satan was given permission by God to start testing the faith of the martyr's right to death. But God had another intention in mind. While this testing was happening, while the martyrs were being executed for public viewing, the effect "was not what [their] enemies expected. [Christs'] followers among the Hellenistic Jews fled from Jerusalem, but began to preach farther afield."[4] The deaths of the martyrs was encouraging the church to go out and spread the gospel to the Roman Empire. Since the empire began to persecute Christians even more, it once again had the opposite effect that Roman Empire had hoped for. "[M]artyrdom serves as proof of the veracity of Christianity, the true philosophy."[5] With the church willingly dying for what they believed in, Satan was meeting with great defeat as the church was growing and being sanctified through the deaths the devil was inflicting on them. Interestingly, when Constantine came to power in 312 AD, the Christian faith moved from being persecuted to the official religion of the Roman Empire. It was still legal to follow the other pagan faiths, but officially, Christianity was the religion of the emperor. Satan was defeated, once again.

There were many different shifts within the Roman church for many centuries. Different groups rose to persecute Christians, most notably among the Muslim nations in the East. Most Muslim warlords allowed Christians to exist among them for a time, but this did change eventually and Christians, to this day are being beheaded and put to death in grisly ways for their faith. Satan is still allowed to persecute the church to their deaths, and yet the gospel grows.

A noticeable time in church history that once again shows the demonic forces trying to persecute those that are wanting to sanctify the church, is the Reformation of Martin Luther and others after him. For centuries the Roman Catholic Church had taught that salvation came through the church. It was the churches' role to impart grace by sacraments and those through the papal priesthood. Luther combated this, particularly once the sale of indulgences began.[6] Luther was incensed that the church became so corrupt to offer salvation for money that he protested against the church by writing the theses, as well as several books. The Roman church would eventually issue a bull condemning the preaching of Luther and all those that sided with him. The pope called on Luther to repent, but he refused, instead burning the bull.[7] The

---

4. Frend, *Martyrdom*, 152.

5. Moss, *Martyrdom*, 98.

6. Bruce L. Shelley, *Church History: In Plain Language* (Nashville, Tennessee: Thomas Nelson, 2013), 250.

7. Shelley, *History*, 247.

Roman Catholic Church would then go on a mission to try and persecute the new Protestants by executing them in public. This once again failed. Satan sought to destroy the Protestant movement, but in the end a sanctifying happened where true faith by grace was once again taught. The idea that grace was given by faith instead of by the sacraments of the church was anathema to the Roman church. This is a doctrine taught by Paul, so Luther was bringing the church back to the sanctifying grace of Christ through the Roman churches' persecutions.

The state of the church today is often thought of with cultural blinders on. To define what that means it is important that many Christians in the North American church are seeing the news reports and news articles in the media as an indicator that the church is in worldwide decline. This is a wrong assumption. True, in the face of the Covid-19 pandemic and the move of extreme social reforms in a time of rising pagan philosophies, it seems like the church is declining in a negative way. The same cannot be said about the church around the world with "[t]he emergence of millions of new, vibrant Christians throughout many sectors of the [w]orld."[8] It is interesting that Patrick Johnstone in his book says that this a world in which "Satan has wrested control."[9] There is an inherent belief that Satan is in control of this world, despite the testimony by someone like Tennent that the church is growing (see his quote). The church is all over the world and engaged in missions. Later Johnstone says that "over the past 20 years ... a growing number of prayer initiatives and networks unprecedented in the history of the world,"[10] are being established all over the world.

The church is growing worldwide. Unfortunately, many churches all over the world have adopted a philosophy of defeatism. The cultural blinders that many Christians in the church have put on are the only thing that makes Satan able to "wrest control" of the world. Satan is testing the Western church and winning. Christians are too invested in themselves to see that through the centuries of testing in other less developed, or unreachable, nations in the world, that God has been sanctifying them and bringing them into the Kingdom of God. Satan is losing in other parts of the world. Satan's testing, even to the point of death, is starting to falter. What is sad is that Satan has convinced many people in North America that he is actually winning when he is not. Satan is wresting control of North America, and many withdrawing churches are handing it to him without a challenge. North American churches are failing the test by God.

To look at the success of the churches ability to pass the testing of Satan that God has allowed the devil to perform, the church in the Western world needs to rethink its point of focus. Throughout history, the church has been attacked right to the point that the church itself is dying and still God is using these demonic tests to sanctify the body of Christ and spread the gospel. The

---

8. Timothy C. Tennent, *Invitation to World Missions: A Trinitarian Missiology for the Twenty-first Century* (Grand Rapids, Michigan: Kregel Academic, 2010), 487.

9. Patrick Johnstone, *The Church is Bigger than you Think: The Unfinished Work of World Evangelism* (Pasadena, California: William Carey Library Publishers, 1998), 270.

10. Johnstone, *Church,* 274.

recent trials of the church with the Covid-19 pandemic is not making the reality that the church is growing in other parts of the world to be noticed. Since the time of the early church when Rome was executing Christians in public, even the mighty Roman emperor was a tool in God's hands to sanctify his church. The persecution and demonic testing was not working, it is time for the church to reclaim that victory in the sanctifying process and realize that Satan needs to be pushed back so that God can be glorified in passing the test he allowed the devil to put the church through.

Chapter VIII - Conclusion

This book has covered a lot of scripture and points in history to prove one biblical point: that Satan needs God's permission to test the church. In doing this, the thesis is made clear about why God allows this testing to occur. The demonic is real and they play an unwilling role in the sanctification of God's church. Christians have assumed for so long that Satan is able to test us and draw the world away at his own autonomous will. The Bible speaks otherwise. Satan cannot operate without God's confirmation. God's sovereignty applies to the demonic as well.

First the theology of where the demonic comes from was considered. The importance of this doctrine gives the church the basis of why demonic creatures have to submit to God's will. Demons do not have the autonomy that Christians often give them. The three theories of demonic origins from a biblical view were considered, as well as a look at the common pagan and occultic origins of the demonic. First, the consideration of whether the demonic come from the souls of a pre-Adamic race from a period between Genesis 1:1 and 1:2 called the "gap theory." This was considered and rejected since there is absolutely no other biblical evidence to back up the claim. Next, the theory of the souls of the Nephilim was given consideration. Once again, it was rejected because it relies too heavily on Second Temple texts that are not considered inspired in any way. Heiser's, Gilbert's and Pitterson's critiques were considered supporting such doctrine, but were found lacking as there is no biblical evidence for the theory but only uninspired texts. The accepted theory was the historic fallen angel's theory as the most likely since it can be supported biblically. Lastly, the pagan occultic origins of demons as children of the demon Lilith was considered and once again rejected since the Bible clearly speaks of a different origin for demons and discounts these claims.

The first piece of evidence of the thesis was an exegesis of Job 1-2:10 and Job 42. In these texts it was shown that Satan came before God and God point-ed out Job to Satan to consider Job's righteousness. Satan questioned this righteousness and God accepted the wager offered by Satan and allowed Satan to first destroy Job's family and sources of prosperity. When Job did not commit apostasy or curse God in any way, Satan once again accused God of protecting Job and if Satan could afflict Job's flesh, then Job would curse God. Job would still not reject God, even at the plea of his own wife. Satan was eventually proven to be wrong, and God was aware that Job would not submit to the pressure to curse God. In the last chapter of Job, it shows that Job did in a sense repent and God blessed him with a greater sanctification. While this blessing was shown in material blessings, it is not the standard that the Bible wants to explain. The further sanctification of God was shown to be Job's acceptance by God. Satan was used in this test to further the sanctification of Job, and he was used unwillingly to do so.

Then the passage of Luke 22:31-38 was looked at. This passage is often looked at by modern Bible readers that it was only Peter being sifted "like wheat" by Satan, but it was in fact all the apostles. Peter was just the leader that was to lead his fellow apostles to remain faithful and persevere in sanctification for the glory of God and the gospel of Christ. Within the exegesis it was noted that the Greek clearly points out that all the apostles were targets of the sifting and that Satan had specifically requested that he be able to do so. Even though the narrative shifts to speaking just of Peter there is still a notion that all the apostles were targets of Satan. Unlike with Job, this "sifting" could lead up to Satan claiming the lives of the apostles. In all but one case, the apostle John, all the apostles were martyred. Only John died of natural causes. Peter was the main target of the exegesis and Jesus did tell Peter that in that very night, he would deny Christ. While Peter was once again to fail the sifting in Galatians with Paul, this sifting was not to cause him to commit apostasy. Eventually Peter would become such an influential voice in the church of Rome that people thought he was the founder of Christianity for hundreds of years afterwards. The sanctification that Peter underwent until the day he was crucified upside down is evident in history. Satan lost Peter in that Peter did not commit apostasy. Instead, Satan had to kill him.

Then a shift happened where the book went back to reconsider texts in the Old Testament. The first was 1 Kings 22:13-28 where Micaiah is called upon to prophesy for Ahab and Jehoshaphat to succeed in their military campaign. Micaiah at first agrees with the false prophets that Ahab will be victorious. Realizing the insult, Ahab calls on Micaiah to tell the truth. So, the prophet of God tells Ahab that God had a demon fill the mouths of the false prophets with lies. These lies were to test Ahab and give him one last opportunity to fall at the feet of the God of Israel. Since God knew that Ahab would not do so, this was a test of condemnation. God was using a demonic creature to once and for all end the rule of what is often considered the most evil king of the northern kingdom. In fury, Ahab imprisoned Micaiah and only ordered him to be released if Ahab is victorious. Ahab ends up dying and Micaiah is justified when he says that if Ahab does not die, then his mouth was filled with lies. Ahab, who was tested by a demonic creature, failed miserably, was killed and brought to justice by the God of Israel that he had rejected his whole life.

The last biblical text that was exegeted was the text of Zechariah 3. In this narrative, a vision of a trial in heaven is shown. Joshua, who represents the remnant of Judah, is brought to trial as an unclean and filthy person. The sins of the people of Judah make them unable to stand before the God of Israel and Judah. Satan goes to accuse Joshua but the angel of the Lord, by Yahweh himself, rebukes Satan and does not allow Satan to bring any accusation or test against the remnant of the people of God. Instead, God reaches down, and makes Joshua clean and sanctifies him for service to God once more. This is important because within the sanctifying process, God commissions Joshua to lead the people of Judah in place of the Davidic king. In doing this political role faithfully, God would bring the Branch, a reference to the coming Messiah. The reason that Satan's accusations and tests were rejected is made clear. Not by passing a test by their own power could Judah, or Joshua, be made holy enough to have the Messiah be born in their line. God was the one that needed to step in, fulfill the promises he had made to the remnants' ancestors, or even some older Jews who were still alive the time of exile, that God would restore them. The accusations of Satan would not be tolerated as God was the only one that could sanctify them for the purpose of bringing forth the Messiah. Satan was stopped from the role as accuser. Satan was rebuked, he had no power to test Joshua, or Judah.

Finally, a look at the history of the church was done. The testing of the church throughout history, from the martyrdom experienced by the Roman Empire, the eventual triumph of the Christian church in that same empire, to the persecution of the Reformation started by Martin Luther that was again a sanctifying call of God. These times of testing, when the threats of death were on the early Christians and newly formed Protestants, it actually did the exact opposite that the Roman Empire and Roman Catholic Church was hoping. These threats, this determination to preach the faith and persevere in the faith caused the faith to grow, and for Protestantism to grow and flourish and bring a sanctifying power to the worldwide church. Satan is considered to have had permission to inflict these tests and to have failed in these situations. With what is going on in the world today, another time of testing is occurring, and the Western church is failing. Cultural blinders are on many churches in North America and because so many negative events are happening in North America, these same churches think this is a worldwide reality. The texts quoted show that it is a belief, but that it simply is not true. The world, and the effort of missions has been tested, and is still being tested by God through Satan, and the church is continuing to grow and evangelize. Since the North American church has accepted a defeatist attitude and withdrawn, it is clear that Satan is "wresting control" of the west and the church needs to step up, and fulfill the Great Commission given to it by Christ.

The evidence of all this exegesis, and historical considerations have shown that Satan cannot perform the testing he is doing without the permission of the sovereign God of heaven. Just like Job, God allows Satan to test his children. Some may think this is cruel or absurd, but the end result is wonderful. Through the testing, if we do not "curse God and die," if we do not fail in our faith in Christ and in the grace of his salvation, then the demonic tests, the abuses we experience in this life, will ultimately bring sanctification in our lives and spirits. To think that the demonic is at our front steps, trying to pry us away from faith in God should not fill Christians with fear. Instead, Christians should be reassured that if God is the one that is using the demonic to test and sanctify us, then it is God that the demonic ultimately need to answer to for what these evil spirits have done to us. Since God is allowing these tests, since God is using the demons in an unwilling way to sanctify us, we can take that as a sense of victory that God is allowing us a moment to have faith and to grow our trust in him in ways that we are not able to do ourselves. Like Hebrews 12:7-10 says that God punishes his own children because he loves them, in the same way, God is testing us, with the most evil beings to exist, in order to sanctify us. God wants to sanctify us because he loves us. That is a great assurance that we can face down this evil and take victory over it.

This should be highly reassuring. The demonic have no power on their own. They are subjected to God in such a way that they really have none of their own autonomy, at least not in the sense that humans do. When God sends them to test and sanctify us, the demonic are most likely presuming that they will be able to break the person they are being sent against. God already knows what the results of this testing and sanctifying will be. Since God is in control, we know that the demons are only able to do to us what God has allowed them to do. This will not last forever. The testing will come to an end. When it does, we will know a sanctification that only a test by God can bring to us. Instead of focusing on why God would use evil creatures like demons to sanctify us, look at it as, God is duping these foolish demons, who think they are getting away with something evil, into doing the will of God. The demons are unwillingly being used by God, to sanctify his church, for his glory.

Epilogue

I have no doubt that some readers having read all this material are now upset with me and the conclusions I have made at times. I honestly do understand. As I hinted at in the Prologue, when I started discovering how much of the spiritual warfare material out there was either unbiblical or total garbage, I was not happy with having been exposed to the truth of God's word. In the end, I ended up rejoicing because I was able to find true freedom in Christ and be able to confidently take shelter in God.

Before I knew the material above, which I knew before the Seminary project, I honestly lived in fear. I was afraid of making one little misstep and having to suffer from demonic issues because of it. At that time, I believed that God gave "me" the authority to free myself from the demonic, and so had that bit of false reassurance, but I was still wary about "new" things. There are many "lists" of stuff out there from charismatic leaning pastors and churches that I took seriously and tried to avoid all the things on the list that I was similarly convicted by. To be fair, somethings on those lists are legitimately things every Christian of any persuasion needs to stay away from, but there were and are still things on those lists that are again existential in nature rather than proving them biblically to be wrong.

After having done the research that led to this paper being suggested in the first place, I felt secure in who God really was as saviour and king. Since Christ is sovereign and I bow to him as Κύριος (Lord), I have nothing to fear from the demonic. This does not give me or you freedom to do anything we desire. God can still use the demonic in judgment of arrogance and pride. However, if God is the one that is placing that judgment on us, if we repent and call on the name of the Lord, he will save us.

A warning I want to issue you the reader is that the Bible never commands us to go "demon hunting". I have heard of young people and even some mature adults that go around looking for demons to exorcise. Some of these individuals have even expected that demon exorcisms should be a regular part of Sunday morning liturgy. This belief has always bothered me. No one in the Bible, not even Christ, went out looking for demons to cast out. The demonic did come to Christ, the young woman diviner even followed Paul around yelling that Paul was there to tell people the way to salvation. However, neither Christ nor Paul went looking for demonic oppressed/possessed people. If these suffering individuals came around, the issue was dealt with.

Essentially, do not go looking for problems. Since God is the one that will determine a demonic oppression, in the life of a believer at least, leave it to God to let that person figure it out and come looking for help. If you are out doing normal chores or leisure time and someone that seems like they are suffering from the demonic comes around, again do not just walk up and start trying to exorcise the demon. Again, this will only lead to problems. In these instances, it is best to call a pastor, an elder or even medical professionals to assess the person. We are not specialists in all matters of natural biology. The person that you are convinced is possessed by a demon could honestly be having a genuine medical problem that needs attention and not to be yelled at to have a demon "come out!"

Be aware of situations around you. God is in ultimate control and it is ultimately God that will decide whether a person is freed from these issues. In all things, make sure you show that person the love of Christ. In the end, you may not even need to help a person with a demonic problem as the love of Christ you show to them might be enough to shake the demons' hold on that person.

After reading all the content I honestly do hope you come away with a greater understanding of God's salvation through Christ. The bonds put on us by our past sinful lives are broken and the hordes of demons cannot affect us in any way anymore without the king of heaven and earths' consent. I find that quite reassuring. I am still careful about what activities I engage in so that I do not push God to send judgment on me. God wants us all to live in the freedom of Christ and we need to praise our King for that freedom and protection from evil presences we cannot even see.

God is good!

Appendix - "I rebuke you Satan in Jesus' name!" ... wait ... is this biblical?

This was originally a post I made on my Reformed Demonology blog on Substack. With the topic that was dealt with in the main part of the thesis of this book, I wanted to be able to offer a helpful suggestion of how to deal with a legitimately demonic possession/oppression. While Christians cannot be possessed, in my biblical convictions, oppression is still quite common and possible if God allows it. Since God does allow it, we are required to recognize it, repent of the sin that may have allowed God to make this happen, and do what biblically has to be done to remove the demonic from our lives. We need to recognize, however, that the demonic oppression on our lives, may not be removed no matter how many times you scream, "IN JESUS' NAME!" at it. The reasons are given below that come from a direct exegesis of the Koine Greek.

***

Many different "spiritual warfare" ministries have been active for decades moving this idea that when "delivering" someone from demonic possession/oppression that the "victim", or exorcist needs to rebuke Satan/the demon in the name of Christ for the evil spirit to be removed.[1]

The question is: is this biblical? The verse that is often used as a proof text for this "doctrine" is Jude 9: "But when the archangel Michael, contending with the devil, was disputing about the body of Moses, he did not presume to pronounce a blasphemous judgment, but said, 'The Lord rebuke you.'" (Jude 9 ESV) It would seem that this is exactly what the verse is implying.

But the problem is, the Greek seems to be saying something different. This may shock some of you. The problem with English translations and the many different versions we have now is that many Christians assume the English is as emphatic or implies the same things as the original Koine Greek. The problem is our modern-day English simply does not carry over all the implications of many Greek words.

Some may think that a statement like this is ridiculous. Before such an assumption is made, a look at the text needs to be done.

Before we go to the actual text of "The Lord rebuke you!" there is something else we need to take into consideration beforehand. This has to do with the identity of Michael. Simply, this blog, overall deals more with demonology and the occult, rather than its parent category, angel-

---

1. John Eckhardt, *Deliverance and Spiritual Warfare Manual* (Lake Mary, Florida: Charisma House, 2014), 70.

ology. However, some may raise the argument that it changes the effects of the text below and I want to show that it really does not.

The first thought of Michael is the fairly traditional one. That Michael is nothing more than an "archangel" or the prince of heaven, meaning the head of the angels. Texts that seem to say this are in Daniel 10:13, 21, 12:1 and Revelation 12:7. These texts do describe Michael as an angel. Many Christians hammer this fact home as the final answer. Angels are created beings and are not in any way divine.

There is something else to consider, however. If all angels are created beings, that none are divine, then what about the "angel of the LORD"? Many over church history have argued that this "angel" is the pre-incarnate Christ. If that is true, then why is this "angel' described as the "malak" (angel/messenger) of Yahweh?[2] That is a good question. When reading the texts that non-Jesus Michael adherents refer to, it clearly shows that Michael will deliver Israel and not just Israel but "Yahweh's people". This is clearly only something Christ or God could do (Daniel 12:1-4). Not an angel.

So, does this mean that I believe Michael in Jude is a synonym for Christ? Actually, I am not fully convinced. For the most part, I am convinced that Michael is exactly as the text says, an archangel. We must realize however that there are other, legitimate ways of looking at who Michael is. If someone rejects that Michael cannot be a synonym for Christ because his is called an "angel", then sorry, you cannot justify that the angel of the Lord is the pre-incarnate Christ. Terms do not change meaning in the Bible simply because you need them to.[3]

I could continue in this train of thought, but that is a topic for angelology and Christology, rather than demonology. There is another proof text for Michael being Christ coming out of Zechariah 3 since the incidents are so similar. Once again, this line of argument requires the belief that the angel of the Lord is Christ. There is an argument that the angel may actually not be.[4] Again, that is a topic for another theologian to deal with elsewhere.

Now then, we need to take a closer look at the actual Koine Greek of the statement, "The Lord rebuke you." Here is the Koine Greek form of that statement: Ἐπιτιμήσαι σοι κύριος,[5] this may look like nonsense to some, so I will transliterate, Epitimēsai soi kyrios. So, what word in there do we as Christian demonologists (spiritual warfare) need to focus on? That would be: epitimēsai. The lexical (the form you have to know to look it up in the Greek dictionary) is the word that means "to rebuke".[6] The other indicators of this verb is that it is active and aorist.[7] That means that it is a past active action

---

2. S. A. Meier, "Angel of Yahweh," in *Dictionary of Deities and Demons in the Bible*, ed. Karel van der Toorn, Bob Becking, and Pieter W. van der Horst (Leiden: Brill, 1999), 53-59.

3. M. Mach, "Michael," in *Dictionary of Deities and Demons in the Bible*, ed. Karel van der Toorn, Bob Becking, and Pieter W. van der Horst (Leiden: Brill, 1999), 569-572.

4. See Footnote 2.

5. Kurt Aland et al., *The Greek New Testament, Fourth Revised Edition (with Morphology)* (Deutsche Bibelgesellschaft, 2006), Jude 9.

6. Henry George Liddell et al., *A Greek-English Lexicon* (Oxford, United Kingdom: Clarendon Press, 1996), 666–667.

that is also finished. So, the completed action is no longer happening, basically it happened then and at that moment. Not in any way pushing into the future.

However, there is another part of this verb that cannot be overlooked. In the form the verb is found in Jude 9, it is an optative verb. Those who are not familiar with the original Greek will probably look confused at that term. It means that it is a "possible" action. So, the rebuke is something that "could" happen.[8]

What?

We need to break this down some more to understand. There are seventy places in the New Testament that optative verbs are used. Jude 9 is one, and another is in Romans 6:15. Here this mood (optative) is used for Paul to ask whether we should continue sinning so that grace may abound. Paul says: "by no means!" The optative here indicates what is known as a "negative optative". In layman's English, that indicates an action that should not take place, but it could. In other words, Paul is saying this kind of sinning should not be happening, but Paul knows full well that it will happen in certain circumstances in sinful error.

The text in Jude 9 that we are looking at, is known as a "positive optative". In other words, an action that will probably take place, but there is still a chance it will not.

Imagine it this way: you are having an argument with someone, and that person says something you find ridiculous or non-sensical and you tell them to "go away!" There is a reasonable expectation that the person you are arguing with may not actually go. You hope they will, but there is a chance they will not.

Okay, so what does that have to do with the title of this article? Remember these "deliverance" people (a term I actually do not like) are claiming to do this "in Jesus' name." While this seems appropriate, the earlier part of the verse indicates that Michael did not want to pronounce a blasphemy by rebuking the devil himself. In other words, Michael had to ask Jesus to rebuke the devil. When Michael asked for Christ to issue that rebuke, Michael flat-out recognized that whether Satan was rebuked in that instance was completely up to Jesus, not Michael, and certainly not you.

Returning to the explanation above about Michael, does this affect this rebuke? Not really. The identification is that Jesus is still recognizing that he, the kyrios (Lord), is the one to determine that such a rebuke will happen. So, whether Michael is an angel, or he is Christ, in both circumstances it is recognized that the power to rebuke belongs to Christ alone and no one else.

A critique of this is bound to come from those that will quote Matthew 10:1. In this text, Jesus gives the disciples his authority to cast out unclean spirits (more on this another time) and to heal the sick.[9] Again, the Greek

---

7. William D. Mounce, *Basics of Biblical Greek Grammar*, ed. Verlyn D. Verbrugge and Christopher A. Beetham, Fourth Edition. (Grand Rapids, Michigan: Zondervan, 2019), 241.

8. Daniel B. Wallace, *The Basics of New Testament Syntax: An Intermediate Greek Grammar* (Grand Rapids, Michigan: Zondervan, 2000), 209.

9. R. T. France, *The Gospel of Matthew, The New International Commentary on the New*

speaks loudly as to what Jesus is saying about this authority. A form of the personal pronoun "he" appears three times in this verse alone (each time it is a different spelling but same meaning). It may seem like this "he" would be a natural reading of the text, however, when Greek does that, it is a real emphasis on the "he", that being Christ.

What is being indicated here, is that the authority is still Christ's. Even though Jesus gave the disciples his authority to do these things, it is still Christ's authority and not the apostles to do with as they choose. To assume that they could just walk up to an unclean spirit or someone who is sick and help them and then walk away thinking they used their authority to do it, is to assume something very dangerous.[10] If you are a paid subscriber, you will have read the first post about occultism. At its core the occult believes in self-divination. For the apostles to assume that Jesus' authority was theirs to do with as they wished, and that because Christ gave them that authority that Jesus had to do what they said, is essentially a form of self-divination. If the apostles assumed this thinking, as well as with us, they assumed they could command Christ to do as they want, rather than according to what Jesus wants in his will alone.

The next rebuke some might level is, "well we have the same Spirit as the apostles." This is simply incorrect. There were only ever thirteen apostles: the twelve confirmed in Acts 1:12-26 and Paul. I do not believe that Judas Iscariot was truly an apostle. A disciple? Yes. An apostle? No. The gift of apostleship is gone. Despite what Word-Faith and New Apostolic Reformation (NAR) heretics teach, there will never be any other apostles. That ministry is done and was done when John died in exile (the only apostle to die of natural causes). These thirteen men had more scriptural authority and blessings of the Holy Spirit than anyone today has ever had. If you want proof, simply look at the way these men were able to preach, teach, perform miracles, and even write new scripture that is completely absent today. Miracles, preaching and teaching still happen, but not to the level that the thirteen apostles were able to make it occur.

Now that people are fully angered and upset, it is time to get to the point. Many in Word-Faith, NAR and charismatic churches will convince people to go to "deliverance" (again, I do not like this ambiguous term) ministries where these leaders will start rebuking the apparent demonic themselves. Many leave these sessions feeling good, but weeks, sometimes days later the problems return and are in a majority of cases much worse than if the person had never gone to the "deliverance" session at all.[11]

Why does this happen? To put it simply, these "ministries" are not allowing for Christ to be the one to decide what is best in this situation. The "minister" is assuming their own authority of the situation and trying to force

---

Testament (Grand Rapids, Michigan: Wm. B. Eerdmans Publication Co., 2007), 377.

10. Craig Blomberg, *Matthew, vol. 22, The New American Commentary* (Nashville, Tennessee: Broadman & Holman Publishers, 1992), 168.

11. If you are looking for excellent resources on how this is possible, check out Doreen Virtue's YouTube videos that speak largely about the false spiritual warfare that is happening in these "deliverance" ministries.

Jesus to do their will, rather than Christ's own. Again, this is occultism, and not the true Christian faith.

When these "deliverances" fail, it is common for these ministries to accuse the "deliverer" for not having enough faith. This again, is nonsense. Faith is given by Christ and by God. It is not something we "build" up to the point that we have enough "power" to do something. Everything happens by the will of the triune-God. If a person is struggling with demonic problems, especially a Christian, there is biblical evidence that God allowed that to happen for his own purposes. If a Christian is oppressed (not possessed, regenerate Christian's cannot be possessed) by a demon, that evil spirit is there because God wants it to be. If the evil spirit is not removed when asking for Christ's rebuke, then God has a reason for that evil spirit staying there. Nothing you can do as a "deliverance" minister will be effective at removing it. As the optative rebuke verb indicates, the rebuke is something that will probably happen, but ultimately Christ is the one to determine if the rebuke happens or not.

This is a heavy topic that many people reading this will be unhappy with. Look at the biblical evidence. Like I said at the beginning, we often take our English Bibles to be a "God authorized final version". This is in error. The English translations, yes, are the word of God, but the true word of God, the words God commanded the writers of the Old and New Testaments to write, were not English. Despite what KJV onlyists say, the English is not the final or "corrected" version of the Hebrew, Aramaic and Greek. If you want to learn what an exorcism is supposed to look like, how it is to happen and so forth, you need to go back to the original language. You do not need to go to Bible College or Seminary to get this knowledge. It only takes diligence to truly study the biblical text that God originally gave us through his chosen scripture writers.

There are other things that need to be said from a demonology perspective about the whole "ritual" process used by charismatics and Word-Faith churches in their exorcisms. Rituals simply are not appropriate and not commanded in the Bible. Rituals like the Roman Ritual[12] and others that many charismatic writers have said "need" to happen to exorcise, are too similar to occult rituals and the truth is these rituals are more dangerous than good. Again, I have heard of too many people that submitted to these rituals that ended up becoming much more demonically oppressed than if they had never gone. All this to say in the end, it is best to completely avoid them.

Note:

I would just like to take a minute to recognize a former pastor in these studies, Reverend Wright. He helped me to understand the Michael is Jesus, line of thinking better than anyone. We have had some deep discussions on the topic and while we both came away not convinced of each other's position, I have come to appreciate the arguments.

---

12. Philip T. Welller (trans.), *Roman Ritual Volume II* (Caritas Publishing, 2017).

Just to state as well, although I am not convinced that Michael is a synonym for Jesus or that the angel of the Lord is the pre-incarnate Christ, I am not totally rejecting the idea either. Despite how closely some hold to these views, they simply are not a requirement of the gospel. If you believe or do not believe Michael is Jesus, you are still a Christian. If you believe or do not believe the angel of the Lord is the pre-incarnate Christ, you are still a Christian. All I ask anyone who wants to critique this, is to do a deep study of these issues before commenting. The bibliography and recommendations will lead you to resources where you can research the idea deeper and come to a well considered conclusion.

Bibliography

Aland, Kurt et al. *The Greek New Testament, Fourth Revised Edition (with Morphology)*. Deutsche Bibelgesellschaft, 2006.

Alden, Robert L. *Job, vol. 11, The New American Commentary*. Nashville: Broadman & Holman Publishers, 1993.

Alexander, P. "3 (Hebrew Apocalypse of) Enoch," in *The Old Testament Pseudepigrapha, vol. 1*. Edited by James H. Charlesworth, 223-315. New York, New York: Yale University Press, 1983.

Anderson, F. I. "2 (Hebrew Apocalypse of) Enoch (Late First Century A.D.) Appendix: 2 Enoch in Merilo Pravednoe, A New Translation and Introduction" in *The Old Testament Pseudepigrapha, vol. 1*. Edited by James H. Charlesworth. 91-221. New York, New York: Yale University Press, 1983.

Anderson, Francis I. *Job: An Introduction and Commentary, vol. 14, Tyndale Old Testament Commentaries*. Downers Grove, Illinois: InterVarsity Press, 1976.

Baldwin, Joyce G. *Haggai, Zechariah and Malachi: An Introduction and Commentary, vol. 28, Tyndale Old Testament Commentaries*. Downers Grove, Illinois: InterVarsity Press, 1972.

Beale, G. K. *The Book of Revelation: A Commentary on the Greek Text, New International Greek Testament Commentary*. Grand Rapids, Michigan; W.B. Eerdmans, 1999.

Blomberg, Craig. *Matthew, vol. 22, The New American Commentary*. Nashville: Broadman & Holman Publishers, 1992.

Boda, Mark J. *The Book of Zechariah*. Edited by R. K. Harrison and Robert L. Hubbard Jr.. The New International Commentary on the Old Testament. Grand Rapids, Michigan: W. B. Eerdmans Publishing Company, 2016.

Bockmuehl, Markus. *Simon Peter in Scripture and Memory*: The New Testament Apostle in the Early Church. Grand Rapids, Michigan: Baker Academic, 2012.

Brown, Francis Samuel Rolles Driver, and Charles Augustus Briggs. *Enhanced Brown-Driver-Briggs Hebrew and English Lexicon*. Oxford: Clarendon Press, 1977.

Bruce, F. F. *The Epistle to the Galatians: A Commentary on the Greek Text, New International Greek Testament Commentary*. Grand Rapids, Michigan: W.B. Eerdmans Pub. Co., 1982.

Charles, R. H. (translator), *The Book of Enoch Revised*. Ingersoll, Ontario: Devoted Publishing, 2019.

Clines, David J. *A. Job 1–20, vol. 17, Word Biblical Commentary*. Dallas, Texas: Word, Incorporated, 1989.

---. *Job 38–42, vol. 18B, Word Biblical Commentary*. Nashville, Tennessee: Thomas Nelson, 2011.

Conway, David. *Magic: An Occult Primer*. Newport, Rhode Island: The Witches Almanac LTD, 2016.

Daniels, Kimberly. *The Demon Dictionary Volume One: Know Your Enemy. Learn His Strategies. Defeat Him!* Lake Mary, Florida: Charisma House, 2013.

---. *The Demon Dictionary Volume Two: An Exposé on Cultural Practices, Symbols, Myths, and the Luciferian Doctrine*. Lake Mary, Florida: Charisma House, 2014.

Devries, Simon J. *1 Kings, 2nd ed., vol. 12, Word Biblical Commentary*. Dallas, Texas: Word, Inc, 2003.

Eckhardt, John. *Deliverance and Spiritual Warfare Manual*. Lake Mary, Florida: Charisma House, 2014.

France, R. T. *The Gospel of Matthew, The New International Commentary on the New Testament*. Grand Rapids, MI: Wm. B. Eerdmans Publication Co., 2007.

Frend, W. H. C. *Martyrdom and Persecution in the Early Church: A Study of the Conflict from the Maccabees to Donatus*. Grand Rapids, Michigan: Baker Book House, 1981.

Fries, Jan. *The Seven Names of Lamastu: A Journey through Mesopotamian Magick and Beyond*. London, England: Avalonia, 2016.

Geisler, Norman. *Systematic Theology, Volume Two*. Minneapolis, Minnesota: Bethany House, 2003.

George, Timothy. *Galatians, vol. 30, The New American Commentary*. Nashville, Tennessee: Broadman & Holman Publishers, 1994.

Gilbert, Derek P. *The Second Coming of Saturn: The Great Conjunction, America's Temple, and the Return of the Watchers*. Crane, Missouri: Defender, 2021.

Green, Joel B. *The Gospel of Luke, The New International Commentary on the New Testament*. Grand Rapids, Michigan: Wm. B. Eerdmans Publishing Co., 1997.

Green, Michael. *2 Peter and Jude: An Introduction and Commentary, vol. 18, Tyndale New Testament Commentaries*. Downers Grove, Illinois: InterVarsity Press, 1987.

Grudem, Wayne. *Systematic Theology*. Grand Rapids, Michigan: Zondervan, 1994.

Guiley, Rosemary Ellen. *The Encyclopedia of Demons & Demonology*. New York, New York: Checkmark Books, 2009.

Guthrie, Shandon L. *Gods of This World: A Philosophical Discussion and Defense of Christian Demonology*. Eugene, Oregon: Pickwick Publications, 2018.

Granholm, Kennet. *Embracing the Dark: The Magic Order of the Dragon Rouge - Its Practice in Dark Magic and Meaning Making*. Sarrijärvi, Suomi: Åbo Akademi University Press, 2005.

Hartley, John E. *The Book of Job, The New International Commentary on the Old Testament*. Grand Rapids, Michigan: Wm. B. Eerdmans Publishing Co., 1988.

Heiser, Michael S. *Demons: What the Bible Really Says about the Powers of Darkness*. Bellingham, Washington: Lexham Press, 2020.

---. *The Unseen Realm: Recovering the Supernatural Worldview of the Bible, First Edition*. Bellingham, Washington Lexham Press, 2015.

House, Paul R. *1, 2 Kings, vol. 8, The New American Commentary*. Nashville, Tennessee: Broadman & Holman Publishers, 1995.

Illes, Judika. *Encyclopedia of Spirits: The Ultimate Guide to the Magic of Fairies, Genies, Demons, Ghosts, Gods & Goddesses*. New York, New York: HarperOne, 2009.

Johnstone, Patrick. *The Church is Bigger than you Think: The Unfinished Work of World Evangelism*. Pasadena, California: William Carey Library Publishers, 1998.

King James I. *Daemonologie*. Woodstock, Ontario: Devoted Publishing, 2016.

Klein, George L. *Zechariah, vol. 21B, The New American Commentary*. Nashville, Tennessee: B & H Publishing Group, 2008.

Liddell, Henry George et al. *A Greek-English Lexicon*. Oxford, United Kingdom: Clarendon Press, 1996.

Long, Gary A. *Grammatical Concepts 101 for Biblical Greek: Learning Biblical Greek Grammatical Concepts through English Grammar*. Peabody, MA: Hendrickson Publishers, 2006.

Longman III, Tremper. *Baker Commentary on the Old Testament: Job*. Grand Rapids, Michigan: Baker Academic, 2012.

Mach, M. "Michael," in *Dictionary of Deities and Demons in the Bible*. Edited by Karel van der Toorn, Bob Becking, and Pieter W. van der Horst, 569-572. Leiden: Brill, 1999.

Marshall, I. Howard. *The Gospel of Luke: A Commentary on the Greek Text, New International Greek Testament Commentary*. Exeter: Paternoster Press, 1978.

Meier, S. A. "Angel of Yahweh." In *Dictionary of Deities and Demons in the Bible*. Edited by Karel van der Toorn, Bob Becking, and Pieter W. van der Horst, 53-59. Leiden, Netherlands: Brill, 1999.

Meier, S. A. "Angels, Messengers, Heavenly Beings." In *Dictionary of the Old Testament: Prophets*. Edited by Mark J. Boda and Gordon J. McConville, 25-26. Downers Grove, Illinois: IVP Academic; InterVarsity Press, 2012.

Morris, Leon. *Luke: An Introduction and Commentary, vol. 3, Tyndale New Testament Commentaries*. Downers Grove, Illinois: InterVarsity Press, 1988.

Moss, Candida R. *Ancient Christian Martyrdom: Diverse Practices, Theologies, and Traditions.* London, England: Yale University Press, 2012.

Mounce, William D. *Basics of Biblical Greek: Grammar Fourth Edition.* Grand Rapids, Michigan: Zondervan, 2019.

Murphy, Edward F. *Handbook for Spiritual Warfare.* Nashville, Tennessee: Thomas Nelson, 1996.

Newman, Albert H. "Introductory Essay on the Manichæan Heresy," in *The Writings Against the Manichaeans and Against the Donatists Part I - The Manichaeans.* Edited by Philip Schaff, 13-44. Ingersoll, Ontario: Devoted Publishing, 2019.

Nolland, John. *Luke 18:35–24:53, vol. 35C, Word Biblical Commentary.* Dallas, Texas: Word, Incorporated, 1993.

Pitterson, Ryan. *Judgment of the Nephilim.* New York, New York: Days of Noe Publishing, 2017.

Rexine, J. E. "Daimōn in Classical Greek Literature." *Greek Orthodox Theological Review 30.3* (1985): 335–61.

Rydberg, Viktor. *Roman Legends about the Apostles Paul and Peter.* Translated by Ottilia Von Düben. London, England: Elliot Stock, 1898.

Schreiner, Thomas R. *1, 2 Peter, Jude, vol. 37, The New American Commentary.* Nashville, Tennessee: Broadman & Holman Publishers, 2003.

Shelley, Bruce L. *Church History: In Plain Language.* Nashville, Tennessee: Thomas Nelson, 2013.

Sinistrari of Ameno. *Demoniality: Incubi and Succubi.* Mockingbird Press LLC. Kindle.

Stein, Robert H. *Luke, vol. 24, The New American Commentary.* Nashville, Tennessee: Broadman & Holman Publishers, 1992.

Tennent, Timothy C. *Invitation to World Missions: A Trinitarian Missiology for the Twenty-first Century.* Grand Rapids, Michigan: Kregel Academic, 2010.

Thompson, Leonard. *Demons.* Joplin, Missouri: College Press Publishing Company, 2005.

Trites, Allison A., William J. Larkin. *Cornerstone Biblical Commentary, Vol 12: The Gospel of Luke and Acts.* Carol Stream, Illinois: Tyndale House Publishers, 2006.

Turner, David and Darrell L. Bock. *Cornerstone Biblical Commentary, Vol 11: Matthew and Mark.* Carol Stream, IL: Tyndale House Publishers, 2005.

Unger, Merrill F. *Biblical Demonology: A Study of Spiritual Forces at Work Today.* Grand Rapids, Michigan: Kregel Publications, 1994.

Uyl, Anthony (editor). *The Book of Jasher.* Woodstock, Ontario: Devoted Publishing, 2017.

Wallace, Daniel B. *The Basics of New Testament Syntax: An Intermediate Greek Grammar.* Grand Rapids, MI: Zondervan, 2000.

Weller, Philip T. (trans.). *Roman Ritual Volume II*. Caritas Publishing, 2017.

Wikipedia. *Alphabet of Sirach*. Wikipedia, last updated October 23, 2021. https://en.wikipedia.org/wiki/Alphabet_of_Sirach.

Wink, Walter. "The World Systems Model." In *Understanding Spiritual Warfare: Four Views*. Edited by Gareth Higgins. Grand Rapids, Michigan: Baker Academic, 2012.

Wiseman, Donald J. *1 and 2 Kings: An Introduction and Commentary, vol. 9, Tyndale Old Testament Commentaries*. Downers Grove, Illinois: InterVarsity Press, 1993.

Zomer, Elyze. "Demons and Tutelary Deities from Heaven", in *Was vom Himmel kommt*. Edited by Gosta Gabirl, Brit Karger, Annette Zgoll and Christian Zgoll, 161-187. Berlin, Germany: DeGruyter, 2021.

Recommended Books

Brueggemann, Walter. *Genesis, Interpretation, a Bible Commentary for Teaching and Preaching.* Atlanta, Georgia: John Knox Press, 1982.

Hamilton, Victor P. *The Book of Genesis, Chapters 1–17, The New International Commentary on the Old Testament.* Grand Rapids, Michigan: Wm. B. Eerdmans Publishing Co., 1990.

Kidner, Derek. *Genesis: An Introduction and Commentary, vol. 1, Tyndale Old Testament Commentaries.* Downers Grove, Illinois: InterVarsity Press, 1967.

Koch, Kurt, *Demonology Past And Present: Identifying and Overcoming Demonic Strongholds.* Grand Rapids, Michigan: Kregel Publications, 2000.

Koch, Kurt. *Occult ABC: Exposing Occult Practices and Bondage.* Grand Rapids, Michigan: Kregel Publications, 1978.

Kraft, Charles H. *Defeating Dark Angels: Breaking Demonic Oppression in the Believer's Life.* Grand Rapids, Michigan: Chosen.

Martin, Walter et al. *The Kingdom of the Occult.* Nashville, Tennessee: Thomas Nelson, 2008.

Mathews, K. A. *Genesis 1-11:26, vol. 1A, The New American Commentary.* Nashville, Tennessee: Broadman & Holman Publishers, 1996.

Unger, Merrill Frederick. *What Demons Can Do to Saints.* Chicago, Illinois: Moody Publishers, 1991.

Waltke, Bruce K. *Genesis: A Commentary.* Grand Rapids, Michigan: Zondervan Academic, 2001.

Walton, John H. *Genesis: The NIV Application Commentary.* Grand Rapids, Michigan: Zondervan, 2001.

Wenham, Gordon J. *Genesis 1–15, vol. 1, Word Biblical Commentary.* Dallas, Texas: Word, Incorporated, 1987.

www.ingramcontent.com/pod-product-compliance
Lightning Source LLC
Chambersburg PA
CBHW061146170426
43209CB00011B/1576